THE AUTHOR

William Hazlitt was born in Maidstone, Kent, in 1778, the son of a Unitarian minister, William, and Grace Hazlitt, both radical intellectuals. The family emigrated first to Ireland, then, in 1783, to America, but returned five years later to settle in Shropshire where – except for a brief period at the Unitarian College in Hackney in 1793 – William grew up.

In 1798 Hazlitt met Coleridge and Wordsworth, a turning point in his life, and left home to study painting in London. He also began to write, publishing *An Essay on the Principles of Human Action* in 1805. In 1808 he married Sarah Stoddart, with whom he had one son. After 1812, when he started writing for the *Morning Chronicle*, he became a well-known journalist and critic: his essays from *The Examiner*, dedicated to his friend Charles Lamb, were published as *The Round Table* in 1817, and his other early works include *Characters of Shakespeare's Plays* (1817), *A View of the English Stage* (1818), *English Comic Writers* (1819), and *Dramatic Literature in the Age of Elizabeth* (1820). He also published *Political Essays* (1819-22) and *Table Talk* (1821-22). While writing this last collection he was living through his disastrous infatuation with Sarah Walker, immortalised in *Liber Amoris* (1823).

Hazlitt's later works include more criticism of literature and art, in collections such as *The Spirit of the Age*, or *Contemporary Portraits* (1825). His last completed project was the massive *Life of Napoleon Buonaparte* (1828-30), and when he died he was working on a life of Titian. In 1824 Hazlitt married Isabella Bridgewater, and they set off for Italy, but she left him on the way home. He became increasingly ill and impoverished, but continued to write until his death from cancer in London in 1830.

LIBER AMORIS
or
The New Pygmalion

William Hazlitt

New Introduction by
Michael Neve

THE HOGARTH PRESS

LONDON

Published in 1985 by
The Hogarth Press
Chatto & Windus Ltd
40 William IV Street, London WC2N 4DF

First published in Great Britain in 1823
Hogarth edition offset from Elkin Mathews and John Lane edition 1893
Introduction copyright © Michael Neve 1985

British Library Cataloguing in Publication Data

Hazlitt, William
Liber amoris, or, The new pygmalion.
1. Hazlitt, William 2. Authors, English –
19th century – Biography
I. Title
824'.7 PR4773
ISBN 0 7012 1018 4

Printed in Great Britain by
Cox & Wyman Ltd
Reading, Berkshire

CONTENTS

INTRODUCTION

Sulking, moodiness and violent obsession are not customarily thought of as handmaidens to the production of vivid, vulnerable masterpieces of passion and loss, but such is the case with William Hazlitt's *Liber Amoris*, which first appeared, anonymously, in 1823. By many of the more conservative readers of Hazlitt's work, *Liber Amoris* has often been seen as an unfortunate débâcle in the career of this famous critic, painter and sports fan, an ugly excrescence in the middle life of a sensitive student of Shakespeare's plays and England's picture galleries. But as so often in the literature of Romanticism, hidden depths come to reveal themselves, and behind Hazlitt's heightened dialogue – one which obsession reduces to a monologue – lies a subtle, yet direct and powerful meditation on the philosophical ludicrousness of love itself. Through conversation, letters to friends about conversations (and sightings), through the use of literary asides, Hazlitt composes an exquisite, finished picture of driven desire, a desire that, with Freudian exactness, ends up without even an obscure object. Instead, we have the *Liber Amoris*.

The edition reproduced here is that published by Elkin Mathews and John Lane in 1893 with an introduction by Richard Le Gallienne. The text follows that of 1823 and the introduction (reprinted here as an afterword), which is full of biographical speculation and gossip, gives a good sense of the scandal which surrounded the work on first publication and which endured right up to the Gay Nineties. (Although Le Gallienne argues that *Liber Amoris* reveals a vital part of Hazlitt's temperament, he still sees the book as an aberration, a product of weakness.) The 1893 edition is also interesting in that it began to draw together in the appendices some of the scattered background material to the book's creation. For in

1823 Hazlitt had published a meditation on love and art that was distilled with the assurance of a painter from a quite extraordinarily violent chaos of unruly feelings. Much fuller and more precise material has been collected as the years have gone by (see the Publisher's Note at the end of this volume) but Le Gallienne started to draw attention to the fact that *Liber Amoris*, although it arose out of a personal crisis, was a carefully planned publication and not an indulgent, confessional outpouring. Hazlitt has given us, as it were, a pictorial account of obsession, and not a vulgar advertisement that expects attention for merely sounding off about it.

The early 1820s were a bad time for Hazlitt. In 1822, at the age of forty-four, his first marriage had broken down, and Hazlitt was to set off for Scotland (what Cyril Connolly called in his essay on *Liber Amoris* "the indifferent Reno of the North") to obtain a divorce. Just as important, to a political animal of Hazlitt's temper, the contemporary world itself had entered a shabby state of vacuity, betrayal and reactionary histrionics. Napoleon, hero and champion of progress was, at least in the minds of the trimmers and the agents of corrupt legitimacy, dead. Power, in one way a source of inspiration and hope, had become mere power politics. The poor people of England, instead of bread and the franchise, were to be segregated and abused under the false science of Malthusian political
economy.

Likewise, the first generation of Romantic poets, the heroes of Hazlitt's youth, whom he would walk miles in all weathers to hear, had become part of the politics of reaction. In ways that *Liber Amoris* intends to mock, part of this reaction included a domesticated sexlessness, an emphasis on the cosy interior of family virtue, as part of its idea of the good and true life. No less a figure than the man who made Romanticism possible – William Wordsworth – had become one of its spokesmen. In the midst of this artless half-world, Hazlitt decided to expose himself in public.

For he had become sexually obsessed with someone who

shared his wife's christian name, if not more: one Sarah
Walker, daughter of Hazlitt's landlord at 9 Southampton
Buildings, Holborn. *Liber Amoris* is made up of some of the
recollections and letters that Hazlitt wrote about his unhappy affair, most of them addressed to two male friends,
P.G. Patmore and J.S. Knowles. It would be out of place, in an
introduction, to discuss the dialectical violence that fuels the
1823 edition, but part of Hazlitt's achievement, in his pursuit
of Sarah Walker, is to generalise on the empty-handedness
with which lovers return from Cupid's world, as if love itself,
for the loved one, is unbearably burdensome, and to be fled
from. Hazlitt elsewhere condensed this experience of being
taken to the heart of loss with a favoured quote from (notably)
Don Quixote: "We hunt the wind, we worship the statue, cry
aloud to the desert." Such is love, where absence, in Hazlitt's
view, does not make the heart grow fonder, but instead leads it
to a point beyond control, where the only governing authority
is art itself.

As the best critics of Romantic writing have pointed out,
Liber Amoris is highly literary, full of allusion, and very
theatrical. Hazlitt, that moody fellow sitting alone in the front
stalls, here plays Hamlet and Leontes, Iago and Othello, or
more bookishly, Werther and Lovelace. He adds to this
self-stage management the vivacity (to put it no more strongly)
of the pugilist, a fighter who is capable of both delicate
footwork and angry punches, but who will, in the end, smash
the statue of his love to pieces. Hazlitt calls the audience to the
ringside of his framed obsession, and here (especially the
loathsome Tories from *The Times* and *John Bull*) all will watch
the unbending man of feeling blight his love life, as all great
Shakespeareans should do.

As the three sections of *Liber Amoris* move from fragmentary
dialogue to retrospection, Hazlitt alludes to, plays at, and
mocks a wide range of inherited figures and themes in
literature. He is not only acting out Shakespeare, or finding
himself dreaming of "a damsel with a dulcimer", or awaking,
with all lost, "On the cold hill's side", as in his friend Keats's

"La Belle Dame sans Merci". In brilliant, but concealed ways, Hazlitt's obsession has turned him into the Ancient Mariner, mythic creation of the once-adored Coleridge. But with a difference. Hazlitt would talk not merely of the past, or of sea-serpents, or of loss, or of guilt, but of woman.

Politically, Hazlitt is also expressing his ache for his hero, Napoleon, who stalks the pages of *Liber Amoris*, both as love object and as handsome sexual rival. (This obsession with Napoleon brings Hazlitt close to his great European double, Stendhal, whose *De l'Amour* bears reading alongside Hazlitt.) Philosophically, Hazlitt is casting a slur on the professional business of still taking the "life of the mind" seriously. The mighty powers of the mind, the serious claims and discriminations that attend any philosophical account of it (about which Hazlitt cared *intensely*) are here seen revealed in a different form: as obstacles to sexual intercourse. For the very powers of the mind that Hazlitt, as a young philosopher, impressed by the Scottish school, had wanted to describe and distinguish – sympathy and imagination – and indeed their more grandiloquent definitions as peddled by Coleridge, had come to trap their champions. For Coleridge, the babbling archangel cocooned in salubrious Highgate, the abstract world of ideas had become the equivalent of an insane asylum; the man who had seen further than anyone of his age had, in Hazlitt's eyes, given intellectual seriousness a bad name. For Hazlitt, always drawn to the power of the imagined world and yet wary of its corruptions, the vehicles of mental advance had simply come, like everything else, to get in the way of the actual world.

But in no sense is *Liber Amoris* a work of free-form spontaneity, untrammelled by classical austerities. The modern reader, thanks (if that is the right word) to access to a wider correspondence than was used in either 1823 or later, can glimpse Hazlitt truly out of control, out beyond the careful achievement of this text. Sulking, swearing in the letters to his friends, "bitch", "hell", "the slimy, varnished, marble fiend"; even, in an astonishing coda, asking a strangely titled friend F—— to test Sarah Walker's virginity: these make up what could be called the background, or "underground", to what Hazlitt published in 1823. Surprise at the interrogative violence of these feelings must be matched with admiration for their distillation into something as beautiful as his book.

For Hazlitt was exposing and warning at the same time. Warning his young son, to whom he was devoted, that the supposed merits of authorship and scholarship were fake, and all too ready to degenerate into mere opinion. Exposing the world of talk; whether political, or passionate, or philosophical, it had all led to the great Shakespearean word which for Hazlitt *was* England in the 1820s: nothing. And somewhere, somehow, in ways that are easy to forget, Hazlitt was losing two Sarahs: his uneducable, unreachable landlord's daughter, and his wife.

But all was not lost. Hazlitt may indeed have pummelled his love into the ground, in the boxing ring of his duped imagination; his detractors may even have left before the end of the fight, amazed and disgusted. But in terms of its own authority, the *Liber Amoris* achieves an astonishing coup, and not simply as a work that satirises Romantic ideas of imagination and intellectual authority. One's admiration for the work need not rest with the wry admission by the writer that a sublime landscape cannot be seen properly if the mind is harping on an absent sexual love, itself a spoof (in about three sentences) on volumes of aesthetic theory. First, *Liber Amoris* exists, albeit as a deep irony: the book, not the possession, of love. But Hazlitt had tried for something far greater. In ways that speak for Hazlitt's seriousness and also for his scepticism, he had attempted to help return the issues of the day to first principles, to the actual groundwork of common life, away, in true Baconian fashion, from the cobwebs of theory and death. He, after all, did not die with his publication, but instead went on to an enriched life as a writer, a life where he had earned the right, by sheer intellectual courage, to paint the portrait both of himself and of his age. This courage had very much to do with his loyalty, especially to political ideals, to the actual common social world of work and struggle, and to the belief that the physical world could be manifested in art without betraying its ordinariness or its palpability. Metaphysics, which now included an exaggerated expectation of sexual happiness, was a delusion. It is the essential point of Hazlitt's importance that he should, in managing this transition, have produced in the *Liber Amoris* a work that came from within a moment of general defeat, and that the painter's truthfulness, his sense of common beauty, his attempt to reach a democratic erotic moment, should have been construed by most of the senior intelligences of the day as a form of obscenity.

Michael Neve, London 1985

LIBER AMORIS.

PART I.

ADVERTISEMENT.

The circumstances, an outline of which is given in these pages, happened a very short time ago to a native of North Britain, who left his own country early in life, in consequence of political animosities and an ill-advised connection in marriage. It was some years after that he formed the fatal attachment which is the subject of the following narrative. The whole was transcribed very carefully with his own hand, a little before he set out for the Continent in hopes of benefiting by a change of scene, but he died soon after in the Netherlands—it is supposed, of disappointment preying on a sickly frame and morbid state of mind. It was his wish that what

ADVERTISEMENT.

*had been his strongest feeling while living, should
be preserved in this shape when he was no more.—It
has been suggested to the friend, into whose hands
the manuscript was entrusted, that many things
(particularly in the* Conversations *in the first Part)
either childish or redundant, might have been
omitted; but a promise was given that not a word
should be altered, and the pledge was held sacred.
The names and circumstances are so far disguised,
it is presumed, as to prevent any consequences result-
ing from the publication, farther than the amuse-
ment or sympathy of the reader.*

THE PICTURE.

H. Oн! is it you? I had something to shew you—I have got a picture here. Do you know any one it's like?

S. No, Sir.

H. Don't you think it like yourself?

S. No: it's much handsomer than I can pretend to be.

H. That's because you don't see yourself with the same eyes that others do. *I* don't think it handsomer, and the expression is hardly so fine as your's sometimes is.

S. Now you flatter me. Besides, the complexion is fair, and mine is dark.

H. Thine is pale and beautiful, my love, not dark! But if your colour were a little heightened, and you wore the same dress, and your hair were let down over your shoulders, as it is here, it might be taken for a picture of you. Look here, only see how like it is. The forehead is like, with that little obstinate protrusion in the middle; the eyebrows are like, and the eyes are just like yours, when you look up and say—" No—never!"

S. What then, do I always say "No—never!" when I look up?

H. I don't know about that—I never heard you say so but once: but that was once too often for my peace. It was when you told me, "you could never be mine." Ah! if you are never to be mine, I shall not long be myself. I cannot go on as I am. My faculties leave me: I think of nothing, I have no feeling about any thing but thee: thy sweet image has taken possession of me, haunts me, and will drive me to distraction. Yet I could almost wish to go mad for thy sake: for then I might fancy that I had thy love in return, which I cannot live without!

S. Do not, I beg, talk in that manner,

but tell me what this is a picture of.

H.   I hardly know ; but it is a very small and delicate copy (painted in oil on a gold ground) of some fine old Italian picture, Guido's or Raphael's, but I think Raphael's.   Some say it is a Madona ; others call it a Magdalen, and say you may distinguish the tear upon the cheek, though no tear is there.   But it seems to me more like Raphael's St. Cecilia, " with looks commercing with the skies," than anything else.—See, Sarah, how beautiful it is ! Ah ! dear girl, these are the ideas I have cherished in my heart, and in my brain ; and I never found any thing to realize them on earth till I met with thee, my love ! While thou didst seem sensible of my kindness, I was but too happy : but now thou hast cruelly cast me off.

S.   You have no reason to say so : you are the same to me as ever.

H.   That is, nothing.   You are to me every thing, and I am nothing to you.   Is it not too true ?

S.   No.

H. Then kiss me, my sweetest. Oh! could you see your face now—your mouth full of suppressed sensibility, your down-cast eyes, the soft blush upon that cheek, you would not say the picture is not like because it is too handsome, or because you want complexion. Thou art heavenly-fair, my love—like her from whom the picture was taken—the idol of the painter's heart, as thou art of mine! Shall I make a drawing of it, altering the dress a little, to shew you how like it is?

S. As you please.—

THE INVITATION.

H.   But I am afraid I tire you with this prosing description of the French character and abuse of the English ?   You know there is but one subject on which I should ever wish to talk, if you would let me.

S.   I must say, you don't seem to have a very high opinion of this country.

H.   Yes, it is the place that gave you birth.

S.   Do you like the French women better than the English ?

H.   No : though they have finer eyes, talk better, and are better made.   But they none of them look like you.   I like the Italian women I have seen, much better than the French : they have darker eyes, darker hair, and the accents of their native tongue are much richer and more melodious. But I will give you a better account of them when I come back from Italy, if you would like to hear it.

S. I should much. It is for that I have sometimes had a wish for travelling abroad, to understand something of the manners and characters of different people.

H. My sweet girl! I will give you the best account I can—unless you would rather go and judge for yourself.

S. I cannot.

H. Yes, you shall go with me, and you shall go *with honour*—you know what I mean.

S. You know it is not in your power to take me so.

H. But it soon may: and if you would consent to bear me company, I would swear never to think of an Italian woman while I am abroad, nor of an English one after I return home. Thou art to me more than thy whole sex.

S. I require no such sacrifices.

H. Is that what you thought I meant by

sacrifices last night? But sacrifices are no sacrifices when they are repaid a thousand fold.

S. I have no way of doing it.

H. You have not the will.—

S. I must go now.

H. Stay, and hear me a little. I shall soon be where I can no more hear thy voice, far distant from her I love, to see what change of climate and bright skies will do for a sad heart. I shall perhaps see thee no more, but I shall still think of thee the same as ever—I shall say to myself, "Where is she now?—what is she doing?" But I shall hardly wish you to think of me, unless you could do so more favourably than I am afraid you will. Ah! dearest creature, I shall be "far distant from you," as you once said of another, but you will not think of me as of him, "with the sincerest affection." The smallest share of thy tenderness would make me blest; but couldst thou ever love me as thou didst him, I should feel like a God! My face would change to a different expression: my

whole form would undergo alteration. I
was getting well, I was growing young in
the sweet proofs of your friendship: you
see how I droop and wither under your
displeasure! Thou art divine, my love, and
canst make me either more or less than
mortal. Indeed I am thy creature, thy
slave—I only wish to live for your sake—I
would gladly die for you—

S.   That would give me no pleasure.
But indeed you greatly over-rate my power.

H.   Your power over me is that of
sovereign grace and beauty. When I am
near thee, nothing can harm me. Thou art
an angel of light, shadowing me with thy
softness. But when I let go thy hand, I
stagger on a precipice: out of thy sight
the world is dark to me and comfortless.
There is no breathing out of this house:
the air of Italy will stifle me. Go with me
and lighten it. I can know no pleasure
away from thee—

> "But I will come again, my love,
> "An it were ten thousand mile!"

THE MESSAGE.

S. MRS. E—— has called for the book, Sir.

H. Oh! it is there.   Let her wait a minute or two. I see this is a busy-day with you.   How beautiful your arms look in those short sleeves!

S. I do not like to wear them.

H. Then that is because you are merciful, and would spare frail mortals who might die with gazing.

S. I have no power to kill.

H. You have, you have—Your charms are irresistible as your will is inexorable.   I wish I could see you always thus. But I would have no one else see you so. I am jealous of all eyes but my own. I should almost like you to wear a veil, and to be

muffled up from head to foot; but even if
you were, and not a glimpse of you could
be seen, it would be to no purpose—you
would only have to move, and you would be
admired as the most graceful creature in the
world.   You smile—Well, if you were to be
won by fine speeches—

S.   You could supply them!

H.   It is however no laughing matter with
me; thy beauty kills me daily, and I shall
think of nothing but thy charms, till the
last word trembles on my tongue, and that
will be thy name, my love—the name of my
Infelice!   You will live by that name, you
rogue, fifty years after you are dead.   Don't
you thank me for that?

S.   I have no such ambition, Sir.   But
Mrs. E—— is waiting.

H.   She is not in love, like me.   You
look so handsome to-day, I cannot let you
go.   You have got a colour.

S.   But you say I look best when I am
pale.

H.   When you are pale, I think so; but
when you have a colour, I then think you

still more beautiful. It is you that I admire ; and whatever you are, I like best. I like you as Miss L——, I should like you still more as Mrs.——. I once thought you were half-inclined to be a prude, and I admired you as a "pensive nun, devout and pure." I now think you are more than half a coquet, and I like you for your roguery. The truth is, I am in love with you, my angel ; and whatever you are, is to me the perfection of thy sex. I care not what thou art, while thou art still thyself. Smile but so, and turn my heart to what shape you please !

S. I am afraid, Sir, Mrs. E—— will think you have forgotten her.

H. I had, my charmer. But go, and make her a sweet apology, all graceful as thou art. One kiss ! Ah ! ought I not to think myself the happiest of men ?

THE FLAGEOLET.

H. Where have you been, my love!

S. I have been down to see my aunt, Sir.

H. And I hope she has been giving you good advice.

S. I did not go to ask her opinion about any thing.

H. And yet you seem anxious and agitated. You appear pale and dejected, as if your refusal of me had touched your own breast with pity. Cruel girl! you look at this moment heavenly-soft, saint-like, or resemble some graceful marble statue, in the moon's pale ray! Sadness only heightens the elegance of your features. How can I escape from you, when every new occasion, even your cruelty and scorn, brings out some new charm. Nay, your rejection of me, by the way in which you do it, is only a new link added to my chain. Raise those downcast eyes, bend as if an angel stooped, and kiss me....Ah! enchanting little trembler! if such is thy sweetness where thou dost not love, what must thy love have been? I cannot think how any man, having the heart of one, could go and leave it.

S.   No one did, that I know of.

H.   Yes, you told me yourself he left you (though he liked you, and though he knew —Oh! gracious God!—that you loved him) he left you because "the pride of birth would not permit a union."—For myself, I would leave a throne to ascend to the heaven of thy charms. I live but for thee, here—I only wish to live again to pass all eternity with thee. But even in another world, I suppose you would turn from me to seek him out, who scorned you here.

S.   If the proud scorn us here, in that place we shall all be equal.

H.   Do not look so—do not talk so— unless you would drive me mad. I could worship you at this moment. Can I witness such perfection, and bear to think I have lost you for ever ? Oh ! let me hope ! You see you can mould me as you like. You can lead me by the hand, like a little child ; and with you my way would be like a little child's :—you could strew flowers in my path, and pour new life and hope into me. I should then indeed hail the return of spring with joy, could I indulge the faintest hope—would you but let me try to please you !

S.   Nothing can alter my resolution, Sir.

H.   Will you go and leave me so ?

S.   It is late, and my father will be getting impatient at my stopping so long.

H.   You know he has nothing to fear for you—it is poor I that am alone in danger. But I wanted to ask about buying you a flageolet. Could I see that which you have ?   If it is a pretty one, it would hardly be worth while ; but if it isn't, I thought of bespeaking an ivory one for you. Can't you bring up your own to shew me ?

S.   Not to-night, Sir.

H.   I wish you could.

S.   I cannot—but I will in the morning.
H.   Whatever you determine, I must submit to.   Good night, and bless thee!

———

[*The next morning, S. brought up the tea-kettle as usual; and looking towards the tea-tray, she said, "Oh! I see my sister has forgot the tea-pot." It was not there, sure enough; and tripping down stairs, she came up in a minute, with the tea-pot in one hand, and the flageolet in the other, balanced so sweetly and gracefully. It would have been awkward to have brought up the flageolet in the tea-tray, and she could not well have gone down again on purpose to fetch it. Something therefore was to be omitted as an excuse. Exquisite witch! But do I love her the less dearly for it? I cannot.*]

THE CONFESSION.

H. You say you cannot love. Is there not a prior attachment in the case? Was there any one else that you *did* like?

S. Yes, there was another.

H. Ah! I thought as much. Is it long ago then?

S. It is two years, Sir.

H. And has time made no alteration? Or do you still see him sometimes?

S. No, Sir! But he is one to whom I feel the sincerest affection, and ever shall, though he is far distant.

H. And did he return your regard?

S. I had every reason to think so.

H. What then broke off your intimacy?

S. It was the pride of birth, Sir, that would not permit him to think of an union.

H. Was he a young man of rank, then?

S. His connections were high.

H. And did he never attempt to persuade you to any other step?

S. No—he had too great a regard for me.

H. Tell me, my angel, how was it? Was he so very handsome? Or was it the fineness of his manners?

S. It was more his manner: but I can't tell how it was. It was chiefly my own fault. I was foolish to suppose he could ever think seriously of me. But he used to make me read with him—and I used to be with him a good deal, though not much neither—and I found my affections entangled before I was aware of it.

H. And did your mother and family know of it?

S. No—I have never told any one but you; nor I should not have mentioned it now, but I thought it might give you some satisfaction.

H. Why did he go at last?

S. We thought it better to part.

H. And do you correspond ?

S. No, Sir. But perhaps I may see him again some time or other, though it will be only in the way of friendship.

H. My God ! what a heart is thine, to live for years upon that bare hope !

S. I did not wish to live always, Sir—I wished to die for a long time after, till I thought it not right ; and since then I have endeavoured to be as resigned as I can.

H. And do you think the impression will never wear out ?

S. Not if I can judge from my feelings hitherto. It is now some time since,—and and I find no difference.

H. May God for ever bless you ! How can I thank you for your condescension in letting me know your sweet sentiments ? You have changed my esteem into adoration.—Never can I harbour a thought of ill in thee again.

S. Indeed, Sir, I wish for your good opinion and your friendship.

H. And can you return them ?

S. Yes.

H. And nothing more?

S. No, Sir.

H. You are an angel, and I will spend my life, if you will let me, in paying you the homage that my heart feels towards you.

THE QUARREL.

H. You are angry with me?

S. Have I not reason?

H. I hope you have; for I would give the world to believe my suspicions unjust. But, oh! my God! after what I have thought of you and felt towards you, as little less than an angel, to have but a doubt cross my mind for an instant that you were what I dare not name—a common lodging-house decoy, a kissing convenience, that your lips were as common as the stairs—

S. Let me go, Sir!

H. Nay—prove to me that you are not so, and I will fall down and worship you. You were the only creature that ever seemed to love me; and to have my hopes, and all my fondness for you, thus turned to a mockery—it is too much! Tell me why you have deceived me, and singled me out as your victim?

S. I never have, Sir. I always said I could not love.

H. There is a difference between love and making me a laughing-stock. Yet what else could be the meaning of your little sister's running out to you, and saying, "He thought I did not see him!" when I had followed you into the other room? Is it a joke upon me that I make free with you? Or is not the joke rather against *her* sister, unless you make my courtship of you a jest to the whole house? Indeed I do not well see how you can come and stay with me as you do, by the hour together, and day after day, as openly as you do, unless you give it some such turn with your family. Or do you deceive them as well as me?

S. I deceive no one, Sir. But my sister Betsey was always watching and listening when Mr. M—— was courting my eldest sister, till he was obliged to complain of it.

H. That I can understand, but not the

other. You may remember, when your servant Maria looked in and found you sitting in my lap one day, and I was afraid she might tell your mother, you said "You did not care, for you had no secrets from your mother." This seemed to me odd at the time, but I thought no more of it, till other things brought it to my mind. Am I to suppose, then, that you are acting a part, a vile part, all this time, and that you come up here, and stay as long as I like, that you sit on my knee and put your arms round my neck, and feed me with kisses, and let me take other liberties with you, and that for a year together; and that you do all this not out of love, or liking, or regard, but go through your regular task, like some young witch, without one natural feeling, to shew your cleverness, and get a few presents out of me, and go down into the kitchen to make a fine laugh of it? There is something monstrous in it, that I cannot believe of you.

S. Sir, you have no right to harass my feelings in the manner you do. I have

never made a jest of you to any one, but
always felt and expressed the greatest
esteem for you. You have no ground for
complaint in my conduct ; and I cannot
help what Betsey or others do. I have
always been consistent from the first. I
told you my regard could amount to no
more than friendship.

H. Nay, Sarah, it was more than half a
year before I knew that there was an insur-
mountable obstacle in the way. You say
your regard is merely friendship, and that
you are sorry I have ever felt any thing
more for you. Yet the first time I ever
asked you, you let me kiss you : the first
time I ever saw you, as you went out of the
room, you turned full round at the door,
with that inimitable grace with which you
do every thing, and fixed your eyes full
upon me, as much as to say, " Is he
caught ? "—that very week you sat upon my
knee, twined your arms round me, caressed
me with every mark of tenderness consistent with modesty ; and I have not got
much farther since. Now if you did all

this with me, a perfect stranger to you, and without any particular liking to me, must I not conclude you do so as a matter of course with every one?—Or if you do not do so with others, it was because you took a liking to me for some reason or other.

S. It was gratitude, Sir, for different obligations.

H. If you mean by obligations the presents I made you, I had given you none the first day I came. You do not consider yourself *obliged* to every one who asks you for a kiss?

S. No, Sir.

H. I should not have thought any thing of it in any one but you. But you seemed so reserved and modest, so soft, so timid, you spoke so low, you looked so innocent— I thought it impossible you could deceive me. Whatever favors you granted must proceed from pure regard. No betrothed virgin ever gave the object of her choice kisses, caresses more modest or more bewitching than those you have given me a thousand and a thousand times. Could I

have thought I should ever live to believe
them an inhuman mockery of one who had
the sincerest regard for you? Do you think
they will not now turn to rank poison in my
veins, and kill me, soul and body? You
say it is friendship—but if this is friendship,
I'll forswear love. Ah! Sarah! it must be
something more or less than friendship. If
your caresses are sincere, they shew fondness—if they are not, I must be more than
indifferent to you. Indeed you once let
some words drop, as if I were out of the
question in such matters, and you could
trifle with me with impunity. Yet you
complain at other times that no one ever
took such liberties with you as I have done.
I remember once in particular your saying,
as you went out at the door in anger—"I
had an attachment before, but that person
never attempted any thing of the kind."
Good God! How did I dwell on that word
before, thinking it implied an attachment to
me also; but you have since disclaimed
any such meaning. You say you have
never professed more than esteem. Yet

once, when you were sitting in your old
place, on my knee, embracing and fondly
embraced, and I asked you if you could not
love, you made answer, "I could easily say
so, whether I did or not— YOU SHOULD
JUDGE BY MY ACTIONS!" And another time,
when you were in the same posture, and I
reproached you with indifference, you replied in these words, "DO I SEEM INDIFF-
ERENT?" Was I to blame after this to
indulge my passion for the loveliest of her
sex? Or what can I think?

S. I am no prude, Sir.

H. Yet you might be taken for one. So
your mother said, "It was hard if you might
not indulge in a little levity." She has
strange notions of levity. But levity, my
dear, is quite out of character in you. Your
ordinary walk is as if you were performing
some religious ceremony : you come up to
my table of a morning, when you merely
bring in the tea-things, as if you were ad-
vancing to the altar. You move in minuet-
time : you measure every step, as if you were
afraid of offending in the smallest things.

I never heard your approach on the stairs, but by a sort of hushed silence. When you enter the room, the Graces wait on you, and Love waves round your person in gentle undulations, breathing balm into the soul! By Heaven, you are an angel! You look like one at this instant! Do I not adore you—and have I merited this return?

S. I have repeatedly answered that question. You sit and fancy things out of your own head, and then lay them to my charge. There is not a word of truth in your suspicions.

H. Did I not overhear the conversation down-stairs last night, to which you were a party? Shall I repeat it?

S. I had rather not hear it!

H. Or what am I to think of this story of the footman?

S. It is false, Sir, I never did any thing of the sort.

H. Nay, when I told your mother I wished she would'nt **** ** **** ********** (as I heard she did) she said "Oh, there's nothing in that, for Sarah

very often ***** ** *** *" and
your doing so before company is only a
trifling addition to the sport.

S. I'll call my mother, Sir, and she shall
contradict you.

H. Then she'll contradict herself. But
did not you boast you were "very persever-
ing in your resistance to gay young men,"
and had been "several times obliged to
ring the bell?" Did you always ring it?
Or did you get into these dilemmas that
made it necessary, merely by the demureness
of your looks and ways? Or had nothing
else passed? Or have you two characters,
one that you palm off upon me, and another,
your natural one, that you resume when you
get out of the room, like an actress who
throws aside her artificial part behind the
scenes? Did you not, when I was courting
you on the staircase the first night Mr.
C—— came, beg me to desist, for if the
new lodger heard us. he'd take you for a
light character? Was that all? Were you
only afraid of being *taken* for a light character? Oh! Sarah!

S.   I'll stay and hear this no longer.

H.   Yes, one word more.   Did you not love another ?

S.   Yes, and ever shall most sincerely.

H.   Then, *that* is my only hope.   If you could feel this sentiment for him, you cannot be what you seem to me of late.   But there is another thing I had to say—be what you will, I love you to distraction ! You are the only woman that ever made me think she loved me, and that feeling was so new to me, and so delicious, that it " will never from my heart."   Thou wert to me a little tender flower, blooming in the wilderness of my life ; and though thou should'st turn out a weed, I'll not fling thee from me, while I can help it.   Wert thou all that I dread to think—wert thou a wretched wanderer in the street, covered with rags, disease, and infamy, I'd clasp thee to my bosom, and live and die with thee, my love. Kiss me, thou little sorceress !

S.   Never !

H.   Then go :   but remember I cannot live without you—nor I will not.

THE RECONCILIATION.

H. I HAVE then lost your friendship?

S. Nothing tends more to alienate friendship than insult.

H. The words I uttered hurt me more than they did you.

S. It was not words merely, but actions as well.

H. Nothing I can say or do can ever alter my fondness for you—Ah, Sarah! I am unworthy of your love: I hardly dare ask for your pity; but oh! save me—save me from your scorn: I cannot bear it—it withers me like lightning.

S. I bear no malice, Sir; but my brother, who would scorn to tell a lie for his sister, can bear witness for me that there was no truth in what you were told.

H. I believe it; or there is no truth in woman. It is enough for me to know that you do not return my regard; it would be too much for me to think that you did not deserve it. But cannot you forgive the agony of the moment?

S. I can forgive; but it is not easy to forget some things!

H. Nay, my sweet Sarah (frown if you will, I can bear your resentment for my ill behaviour, it is only your scorn and indifference that harrow up my soul)—but I was going to ask, if you had been engaged to be married to any one, and the day was fixed, and he had heard what I did, whether he could have felt any true regard for the character of his bride, his wife, if he had not been hurt and alarmed as I was?

S. I believe, actual contracts of marriage have sometimes been broken off by unjust suspicions.

H. Or had it been your old friend, what do you think he would have said in my case?

S. He would never have listened to any thing of the sort.

H. He had greater reasons for confidence than I have. But it is your repeated cruel rejection of me that drives me almost to madness. Tell me, love, is there not, besides your attachment to him, a repugnance to me ?

S. No, none whatever.

H. I fear there is an original dislike, which no efforts of mine can overcome.

S. It is not *you*—it is my feelings with respect to another, which are unalterable.

H. And yet you have no hope of ever being his ? And yet you accuse me of being romantic in my sentiments.

S. I have indeed long ceased to hope ; but yet I sometimes hope against hope.

H. My love ! were it in my power, thy hopes should be fulfilled to-morrow. Next to my own, there is nothing that could give me so much satisfaction as to see thine realized ! Do I not love thee, when I can feel such an interest in thy love for another ? It was that which first wedded my very soul to you. I would give worlds for a share in a heart so rich in pure affection !

S.   And yet I did not tell you of the circumstance to raise myself in your opinion.

H.   You are a sublime little thing! And yet, as you have no prospects there, I cannot help thinking, the best thing would be to do as I have said.

S.   I would never marry a man I did not love beyond all the world.

H.   I should be satisfied with less than that—with the love, or regard, or whatever you call it, you have shown me before marriage, if that has only been sincere. You would hardly like me less afterwards.

S.   Endearments would, I should think, increase regard, where there was love beforehand; but that is not exactly my case.

H.   But I think you would be happier than you are at present. You take pleasure in my conversation, and you say you have an esteem for me; and it is upon this, after the honey-moon, that marriage chiefly turns.

S.   Do you think there is no pleasure in a single life?

H.   Do you mean on account of its liberty?

S. No, but I feel that forced duty is no duty. I have high ideas of the married state!

H. Higher than of the maiden state?

S. I understand you, Sir.

H. I meant nothing; but you have sometimes spoken of any serious attachment as a tie upon you. It is not that you prefer flirting with "gay young men" to becoming a mere dull domestic wife?

S. You have no right to throw out such insinuations: for though I am but a tradesman's daughter, I have as nice a sense of honour as any one can have.

H. Talk of a tradesman's daughter! you would ennoble any family, thou glorious girl, by true nobility of mind.

S. Oh! Sir, you flatter me. I know my own inferiority to most.

H. To none; there is no one above thee, man nor woman either. You are above your situation, which is not fit for you.

S. I am contented with my lot, and do my duty as cheerfully as I can.

H. Have you not told me your spirits

grow worse every year ?

S. Not on that account : but some dis-appointments are hard to bear up against.

H. If you talk about that, you'll unman me. But tell me, my love,—I have thought of it as something that might account for some circumstances ; that is, as a mere pos-sibility. But tell me, there was not a like-ness between me and your old lover that struck you at first sight ? Was there ?

S. No, Sir, none.

H. Well, I didn't think it likely there should.

S. But there was a likeness.

H. To whom ?

S. To that little image ! *(looking intently on a small bronze figure of Buonaparte on the mantle-piece.)*

H. What, do you mean to Buonaparte ?

S. Yes, all but the nose was just like.

H. And was his figure the same ?

S. He was taller !

[*I got up and gave her the image, and told her it was her's by every right that was sacred. She refused at first to take so valuable a curiosity, and said she would keep it for me. But I pressed it eagerly, and she took it. She immediately came and sat down, and put her arm round my neck, and kissed me, and I said "Is it not plain we are the best friends in the world, since we are always so glad to make it up?" And then I added "How odd it was that the God of my idolatry should turn out to be like her Idol, and said it was no wonder that the same face which awed the world should conquer the sweetest creature in it!" How I loved her at that moment! Is it possible that the wretch who writes this could ever have been so blest! Heavenly delicious creature! Can I live without her?—Oh! no—never— never.*

"What is this world? What asken men to have,
"Now with his love, now in the cold grave,
"Alone withouten any compagnie!"

Let me but see her again! She cannot hate the man who loves her as I do.]

LETTERS TO THE SAME.

Feb. 1822.

—You will scold me for this, and ask me if this is keeping my promise to mind my work. One half of it was to think of Sarah: and besides, I do not neglect my work either, I assure you. I regularly do ten pages a day, which mounts up to thirty guineas' worth a week, so that you see I should grow rich at this rate, if I could keep on so; *and I could keep on so*, If I had you with me to encourage me with your sweet smiles, and share my lot. The Berwick smacks sail twice a week, and the wind sits fair. When I think of the thousand endearing caresses that have passed between us, I do not wonder at the strong

attachment that draws me to you; but I
am sorry for my own want of power to
please. I hear the wind sigh through the
lattice, and keep repeating over and over to
myself two lines of Lord Bryon's Tragedy—

> " So shalt thou find me ever at thy side
> Here and hereafter, if the last may be "—

applying them to thee, my love, and thinking whether I shall ever see thee again.
Perhaps not—for some years at least—till
both thou and I are old—and then, when
all else have forsaken thee, I will creep to
thee, and die in thine arms. You once
made me believe I was not hated by her I
loved; and for that sensation, so delicious
was it, though but a mockery and a dream,
I owe you more than I can ever pay. I
thought to have dried up my tears for ever,
the day I left you; but as I write this, they
stream again. If they did not, I think my
heart would burst. I walk out here of an
afternoon, and hear the notes of the thrush,
that come up from a sheltered valley below,
welcome in the spring; but they do not melt

my heart as they used : it is grown cold
and dead. As you say, it will one day be
colder.—Forgive what I have written above ;
I did not intend it : but you were once my
little all, and I cannot bear the thought of
having lost you for ever, I fear through my
own fault. Has any one called ? Do not
send any letters that come. I should like
you and your mother (if agreeable) to go
and see Mr. Kean in Othello, and Miss
Stephens in Love in a Village. If you will,
I will write to Mr. T——, to send you
tickets. Has Mr. P—— called ? I think I
must send to him for the picture to kiss and
talk to. Kiss me, my best-beloved. Ah !
if you can never be mine, still let me be
your proud and happy slave.

H.

TO THE SAME.

March, 1822.

—You will be glad to learn I have done my work—a volume in less than a month. This is one reason why I am better than when I came, and another is, I have had two letters from Sarah. I am pleased I have got through this job, as I was afraid I might lose reputation by it (which I can little afford to lose)—and besides, I am more anxious to do well now, as I wish you to hear me well spoken of. I walk out of an afternoon, and hear the birds sing as I told you, and think, if I had you hanging on my arm, *and that for life*, how happy I should be—happier than I ever hoped to be, or had any conception of till I knew you. *"But that can*

never be "—I hear you answer in a soft, low
murmur. Well, let me dream of it sometimes—I am not happy too often, except
when that favorite note, the harbinger of
spring, recalling the hopes of my youth,
whispers thy name and peace together in
my ear. I was reading something about
Mr. Macready to-day, and this put me in
mind of that delicious night, when I went
with your mother and you to see Romeo
and Juliet. Can I forget it for a moment—
your sweet modest looks, your infinite propriety of behaviour, all your sweet winning
ways—your hesitating about taking my arm
as we came out till your mother did—your
laughing about nearly losing your cloak—
your stepping into the coach without my
being able to make the slightest discovery
—and oh ! my sitting down beside you
there, you whom I had loved so long, so
well, and your assuring me I had not less-
ened your pleasure at the play by being
with you, and giving me your dear hand to
press in mine ! I thought I was in heaven—
that slender exquisitely turned form con-

tained my all of heaven upon earth; and
as I folded you—yes, you, my own best
Sarah, to my bosom, there was, as you say,
a tie between us—you did seem to me, for
those few short moments, to be mine in all
truth and honour and sacredness—Oh!
that we could be always so—Do not mock
me, for I am a very child in love. I ought
to beg pardon for behaving so ill afterwards,
but I hope the *little image* made it up between
us, &c.

   [*To this letter I have received no answer, not
     a line. The rolling years of eternity will
     never fill up that blank. Where shall I
     be? What am I? Or where have I been?*]

WRITTEN IN A BLANK LEAF OF ENDYMION.

I WANT a hand to guide me, an eye to cheer me, a bosom to repose on; all which I shall never have, but shall stagger into my grave, old before my time, unloved and unlovely, unless S. L. keeps her faith with me.

* * * * * * * * * * * * * *
* * * * * *

—But by her dove's eyes and serpent-shape, I think she does not hate me; by her smooth forehead and her crested hair, I own I love her; by her soft looks and queen-like grace (which men might fall down and worship) I swear to live and die for her!

A PROPOSAL OF LOVE.

(Given to her in our early acquaintance.)

"Oh! if I thought it could be in a woman
(As, if it can, I will presume in you)
To feed for aye her lamp and flames of love,
To keep her constancy in plight and youth,
Outliving beauties outward with a mind
That doth renew swifter than blood decays :
Or that persuasion could but thus convince me,
That my integrity and truth to you
Might be confronted with the match and weight
Of such a winnowed purity in love—
How were I then uplifted!   But, alas,
I am as true as truth's simplicity,
And simpler than the infancy of truth."

TROILUS AND CRESSIDA.

LIBER AMORIS.

PART II.

LETTERS TO C. P——, ESQ.

Bees-Inn.

MY GOOD FRIEND,

Here I am in Scotland (and shall have been here three weeks, next Monday) as I may say, *on my probation*. This is a lone inn, but on a great scale, thirty miles from Edinburgh. It is situated on a rising ground (a mark for all the winds, which blow here incessantly)—there is a woody hill opposite, with a winding valley below, and the London road stretches out on either side. You may guess which way I oftenest walk. I have written two letters to S. L. and got one cold, prudish answer, beginning *Sir*, and ending *From your's truly*, with *Best respects from herself and relations.*

I was going to give in, but have returned an
answer, which I think is a touch-stone. I
send it you on the other side to keep as a
curiosity, in case she kills me by her
exquisite rejoinder. I am convinced from
the profound contemplations I have had on
the subject here and coming along, that I
am on a wrong scent. We had a famous
parting-scene, a complete quarrel and then
a reconciliation, in which she did beguile
me of my tears, but the deuce a one did
she shed. What do you think? She cajoled
me out of my little Buonaparte as cleverly
as possible, in manner and form following.
She was shy the Saturday and Sunday (the
day of my departure) so I got in dudgeon,
and began to rip up grievances. I asked
her how she came to admit me to such
extreme familiarities, the first week I
entered the house. "If she had no particular regard for me, she must do so (or
more) with every one : if she had a liking
to me from the first, why refuse me with
scorn and wilfulness?" If you had seen
how she flounced, and looked, and went to

the door, saying "She was obliged to me
for letting her know the opinion I had
always entertained of her"—then I said,
"Sarah!" and she came back and took my
hand, and fixed her eyes on the mantle-
piece—(she must have been invoking her
idol then—if I thought so, I could devour
her, the darling—but I doubt her)—So I
said "There is one thing that has occurred
to me sometimes as possible, to account
for your conduct to me at first—there wasn't
a likeness, was there, to your old friend?"
She answered "No, none—but there was a
likeness"—I asked, to what? She said
"To that little image!" I said, "Do you
mean Buonaparte?"—She said, "Yes, all
but the nose."—"And the figure?"—"He
was taller."—I could not stand this. So I
got up and took it, and gave it her, and
after some reluctance, she consented to
"keep it for me." What will you bet me
that it wasn't all a trick? I'll tell you why
I suspect it, besides being fairly out of my
wits about her. I had told her mother half
an hour before, that I should take this

image and leave it at Mrs. B.'s, for that I didn't wish to leave any thing behind me that must bring me back again. Then up she comes and starts a likeness to her lover: she knew I should give it her on the spot — "No, she would keep it for me!" So I must come back for it. Whether art or nature, it is sublime. I told her I should write and tell you so, and that I parted from her, confiding, adoring!—She is beyond me, that's certain. Do go and see her, and desire her not to give my present address to a single soul, and learn if the lodging is let, and to whom. My letter to her is as follows. If she shews the least remorse at it, I'll be hanged, though it might move a stone, I modestly think. *(See before, Part I. page* 37*)*.

N.B. I have begun a book of our conversations (I mean mine and the statue's) which I call LIBER AMORIS. I was detained at Stamford and found myself dull, and could hit upon no other way of employing my time so agreeably.

LETTER II.

DEAR P——,

Here without loss of time, in order that I may have your opinion upon it, is little Yes and No's answer to my last.

"SIR,

"I should not have disregarded your injunction not to send you any more letters that might come to you, had I not promised the Gentleman who left the enclosed to forward it the earliest opportunity, as he said it was *of consequence*. Mr. P— called the day after you left town. My mother and myself are much obliged by your kind offer of tickets to the play, but must decline accepting it. My family send their best respects, in which they are joined by

Your's truly,

S. L."

The deuce a bit more is there of it. If

you can make any thing out of it (or any
body else) I'll be hanged. You are to
understand, this comes in a frank, the
second I have received from her, with a
name I can't make out, and she won't tell
me, though I asked her, where she got
franks, as also whether the lodgings were
let, to neither of which a word of answer.
* * * * is the name on the frank: see if you
can decypher it by a Red-book. I suspect
her grievously of being an arrant jilt, to say
no more—yet I love her dearly. Do you
know I'm going to write to the sweet rogue
presently, having a whole evening to myself
in advance of my work? Now mark,
before you set about your exposition of the
new Apocalypse of the New Calypso, the
only thing to be endured in the above letter
is the date. It was written the very day
after she received mine. By this she seems
willing to lose no time in receiving these
letters "of such sweet breath composed."
If I thought so—but I wait for your reply.
After all, what is there in her but a pretty
figure, and that you can't get a word out of

her?   Her's is the Fabian method of making
love and conquests.   What do you suppose
she said the night before I left her?

"H. Could you not come and live with
me as a friend?

S.   I don't know: and yet it would be of
no use if I did, you would always be hankering after what could never be!"

I asked her if she would do so at once—
the very next day?   And what do you guess
was her answer—"Do you think it would
be prudent?"   As I didn't proceed to extre-
mities on the spot, she began to look grave,
and declare off.   "Would she live with me
in her own house—to be with me all day as
dear friends, if nothing more, to sit and
read and talk with me?"—"She would
make no promises, but I should find her the
same."—"Would she go to the play with
me sometimes, and let it be understood that
I was paying my addresses to her?"—"She
could not, as a habit—her father was rather
strict, and would object."—Now what am I
to think of all this?   Am I mad or a fool?
Answer me to that, Master Brook!   You are
a philosopher.

LETTER III.

DEAR FRIEND,

I ought to have written to you before; but since I received your letter, I have been in a sort of purgatory, and what is worse, I see no prospect of getting out of it. I would put an end to my torments at once; but I am as great a coward as I have been a dupe. Do you know I have not had a word of answer from her since! What can be the reason? Is she offended at my letting you know she wrote to me, or is it some new affair? I wrote to her in the tenderest, most respectful manner, poured my soul at her feet, and this is the return she makes me! Can you account for it, except on the admission of my worst doubts concerning her? Oh God! can I bear

after all to think of her so, or that I am
scorned and made a sport of by the creature
to whom I had given my whole heart?—
Thus has it been with me all my life; and
so will it be to the end of it!—If you
should learn any thing, good or bad, tell
me, I conjure you: I can bear any thing
but this cruel suspense. If I knew she
was a mere abandoned creature, I should
try to forget her; but till I do know this,
nothing can tear me from her, I have drank
in poison from her lips too long—alas!
mine do not poison again. I sit and indulge
my grief by the hour together; my weakness grows upon me; and I have no hope
left, unless I could lose my senses quite.
Do you know I think I should like this?
To forget, ah! to forget—there would be
something in that—to change to an ideot
for some few years, and then to wake up a
poor wretched old man, to recollect my
misery as past, and die! Yet, oh! with
her, only a little while ago, I had different
hopes, forfeited for nothing that I know of!
* * * * * * * If you can give me any con-

solation on the subject of my tormentor,
pray do. The pain I suffer wears me out
daily. I write this on the supposition that
Mrs.——may still come here, and that I may
be detained some weeks longer. Direct to
me at the Post-office; and if I return to
town directly as I fear, I will leave word
for them to forward the letter to me in
London—not at my old lodgings. I will
not go back there : yet how can I breathe
away from her ? Her hatred of me must
be great, since my love of her could not
overcome it ! I have finished the book of
my conversations with her, which I told you
of : if I am not mistaken, you will think
it very nice reading.

                              Your's ever.

Have you read Sardanapalus ? How like
the little Greek slave, Myrrha, is to *her* !

LETTER IV.

(Written in the Winter).

MY GOOD FRIEND,

I received your letter this morning, and I
kiss the rod not only with submission, but
gratitude. Your reproofs of me and your
defences of her are the only things that
save my soul from perdition. She is my
heart's idol; and believe me those words of
yours applied to the dear saint—"To lip a
chaste one and suppose her wanton"—were
balm and rapture to me. I have *lipped her*,
God knows how often, and oh! is it even
possible that she is chaste, and that she has
bestowed her loved "endearments" on me
(her own sweet word) out of true regard?
That thought, out of the lowest depths of

despair, would at any time make me strike
my forehead against the stars.   Could I but
think the love "honest," I am proof against
all hazards.   She by her silence makes my
dark hour; and you by your encouragements
dissipate it for twenty-four hours.   Another
thing has brought me to life.   Mrs.——is
actually on her way here about the divorce.
Should this unpleasant business (which has
been so long talked of) succeed, and I
should become free, do you think S. L. will
agree to change her name to —— ?   If she
will, she *shall;* and to call her so to you or
to hear her called so by others, would be
music to my ears, such as they never drank
in.   Do you think if she knew how I love
her, my depressions and my altitudes, my
wanderings and my constancy, it would not
move her ?   She knows it all; and if she is
not an *incorrigible*, she loves me, or regards
me with a feeling next to love.   I don't
believe that any woman was ever courted
more passionately than she has been by me.
As Rousseau said of Madame d'Houptot
(forgive the allusion) my heart has found

a tongue in speaking to her, and I have
talked to her the divine language of love.
Yet she says, she is insensible to it.   Am
I to believe her or you ?   You—for I wish
it and wish it to madness, now that I am
like to be free, and to have it in my power
to say to her without a possibility of suspicion, " Sarah, will you be mine ?"   When
I sometimes think of the time I first saw
the sweet apparition, August 16, 1820, and
that possibly she may be my bride before
that day two years, it makes me dizzy with
incredible joy and love of her.   Write soon.

LETTER V.

MY DEAR FRIEND,

I read your answer this morning with gratitude. I have felt somewhat easier since. It shewed your interest in my vexations, and also that you know nothing worse than I do. I cannot describe the weakness of mind to which she has reduced me. This state of suspense is like hanging in the air by a single thread that exhausts all your strength to keep hold of it; and yet if that fails you, you have nothing in the world else left to trust to. I am come back to Edinburgh about this cursed business, and Mrs. —— is coming from Montrose next week. How it will end, I can't say; and don't care, except as it regards the other affair. I should, I confess, like to have it in my power to make her the

offer direct and unequivocal, to see how she'd
receive it. It would be worth something at
any rate to see her superfine airs upon the
occasion ; and if she should take it into her
head to turn round her sweet neck, drop her
eye-lids, and say—" Yes, I will be yours !"—
why then, " treason domestic, foreign levy,
nothing could touch me further." By Heaven ! I doat on her. The truth is, I never had
any pleasure, like love, with any one but her.
Then how can I bear to part with her ? Do
you know I like to think of her best in her
morning-gown and mob-cap—it is so she has
oftenest come into my room and enchanted
me ! She was once ill, pale, and had lost
all her freshness. I only adored her the more
for it, and fell in love with the decay of her
beauty. I could devour the little witch.
If she had a plague-spot on her, I could
touch the infection : if she was in a burning
fever, I could kiss her, and drink death as I
have drank life from her lips. When I
press her hand, I enjoy perfect happiness
and contentment of soul. It is not what she
says or what she does—it is herself that I

love. To be with her is to be at peace. I
have no other wish or desire. The air about
her is serene, blissful; and he who breathes
it is like one of the Gods! So that I can
but have her with me always, I care for
nothing more. I never could tire of her
sweetness; I feel that I could grow to her,
body and soul? My heart, my heart is her's.

LETTER VI.

(Written in May).

DEAR P———,

What have I suffered since I parted with you! A raging fire is in my heart and in my brain, that never quits me. The steam-boat (which I foolishly ventured on board) seems a prison-house, a sort of spectre-ship, moving on through an infernal lake, without wind or tide, by some necromantic power—the splashing of the waves, the noise of the engine gives me no rest, night or day—no tree, no natural object varies the scene—but the abyss is before me, and all my peace lies weltering in it! I feel the eternity of punishment in this life; for I see no end of my woes. The people about me are ill, uncom-

fortable, wretched enough, many of them—
but to-morrow or next day, they reach the
place of their destination, and all will be new
and delightful. To me it will be the same.
I can neither escape from her, nor from myself. All is endurable where there is a
limit : but I have nothing but the blackness
and the fiendishness of scorn around me—
mocked by her (the false one) in whom I
placed my hope, and who hardens herself
against me !—I believe you thought me quite
gay, vain, insolent, half mad, the night I left
the house—no tongue can tell the heaviness
of heart I felt at that moment. No footsteps
ever fell more slow, more sad than mine ; for
every step bore me farther from her, with
whom my soul and every thought lingered.
I had parted with her in anger, and each had
spoken words of high disdain, not soon to
be forgiven. Should I ever behold her
again ? Where go to live and die far from
her ? In her sight there was Elysium ; her
smile was heaven ; her voice was enchantment ; the air of love waved round her,
breathing balm into my heart : for a little

while I had sat with the Gods at their golden tables, I had tasted of all earth's bliss, " both living and loving ! " But now Paradise barred its doors against me ; I was driven from her presence, where rosy blushes and delicious sighs and all soft wishes dwelt, the outcast of nature and the scoff of love ! I thought of the time when I was a little happy careless child, of my father's house, of my early lessons, of my brother's picture of me when a boy, of all that had since happened to me, and of the waste of years to come— I stopped, faultered, and was going to turn back once more to make a longer truce with wretchedness and patch up a hollow league with love, when the recollection of her words —" I always told you I had no affection for you "—steeled my resolution, and I determined to proceed. You see by this she always hated me, and only played with my credulity till she could find some one to supply the place of her unalterable attachment to *the little image*. * * * * * I am a little, a very little better to-day. Would it were quietly over ; and that this misshapen form (made to be mocked) were hid out of the sight of cold, sullen eyes! The people about me even take notice of my dumb despair, and pity me. What is to be done? I cannot forget *her;* and I can find no other like what *she seemed.* I should wish you to call, if you can make an excuse, and see whether or no she is quite marble—whether I may go back again at my return, and whether she will see me and talk to me sometimes as an old friend. Suppose you were to call on M—— from me, and ask him what his impression is that I ought to do. But do as you think best. Pardon, pardon.

P.S. I send this from Scarborough, where the vessel stops for a few minutes. I scarcely know what I should have done, but for this relief to my feelings.

LETTER VII.

MY DEAR FRIEND,

The important step is taken, and I am virtually a free man. * * * What had I better do in these circumstances? I dare not write to her, I dare not write to her father, or else I would. She has shot me through with poisoned arrows, and I think another "winged wound" would finish me. It is a pleasant sort of balm (as you express it) she has left in my heart! One thing I agree with you in, it will remain there for ever; but yet not very long. It festers, and consumes me. If it were not for my little boy, whose face I see struck blank at the news, looking through the world for pity and meeting with contempt instead, I should soon, I fear, settle the question by my death.

That recollection is the only thought that
brings my wandering reason to an anchor;
that stirs the smallest interest in me; or
gives me fortitude to bear up against what
I am doomed to feel for the *ungrateful*.
Otherwise, I am dead to every thing but
the sense of what I have lost.   She was my
life—it is gone from me, and I am grown
spectral !   If I find myself in a place I am
acquainted with, it reminds me of her, of
the way in which I thought of her,

> —— " and carved on every tree
> The soft, the fair, the inexpressive she ! "

If it is a place that is new to me, it is desolate, barren of all interest ; for nothing
touches me but what has a reference to her.
If the clock strikes, the sound jars me ; a
million of hours will not bring back peace
to my breast.   The light startles me ; the
darkness terrifies me.   I seem falling into a
pit, without a hand to help me.   She has
deceived me, and the earth fails from under
my feet : no object in nature is substantial,
real, but false and hollow, like her faith on
which I built my trust.   She came (I knew

not how) and sat by my side and was folded
in my arms, a vision of love and joy, as if
she had dropped from the Heavens to bless
me by some especial dispensation of a favouring Providence, and make me amends
for all; and now without any fault of mine
but too much fondness, she has vanished
from me, and I am left to perish. My heart
is torn out of me, with every feeling for
which I wished to live. The whole is like a
dream, an effect of enchantment; it torments me, and it drives me mad. I lie down
with it; I rise up with it; and see no chance
of repose. I grasp at a shadow, I try to
undo the past, and weep with rage and pity
over my own weakness and misery. I spared
her again and again (fool that I was) thinking what she allowed from me was love,
friendship, sweetness, not wantonness. How
could I doubt it, looking in her face, and
hearing her words, like sighs breathed from
the gentlest of all bosoms? I had hopes,
I had prospects to come, the flattery of
something like fame, a pleasure in writing,
health even would have come back with her

smile—she has blighted all, turned all to poison and childish tears. Yet the barbed arrow is in my heart—I can neither endure it, nor draw it out; for with it flows my life's-blood. I had conversed too long with abstracted truth to trust myself with the immortal thoughts of love. *That S. L. might have been mine, and now never can*— these are the two sole propositions that forever stare me in the face, and look ghastly in at my poor brain. I am in some sense proud that I can feel this dreadful passion — it gives me a kind of rank in the kingdom of love—but I could have wished it had been for an object that at least could have understood its value and pitied its excess. You say her not coming to the door when you went is a proof—yes, that her complement is at present full! That is the reason she doesn't want me there, lest I should discover the new affair— wretch that I am! Another has possession of her, oh Hell! I'm satisfied of it from her manner, which had a wanton insolence in it. Well might I run wild when I received no letters from her. I foresaw, I felt my fate. The gates of Paradise were at once open to me too, and I blushed to enter but with the golden keys of love! I would die; but her lover—my love of her—ought not to die. When I am dead, who will love her as I have done? If she should be in misfortune, who will comfort her? When she is old, who will look in her face, and bless her? Would there be any harm in calling upon M——, to know confidentially if he thinks it worth my while to make her an offer the instant it is in my power? Let me have an answer, and save me, if possible, *for* her and *from* myself.

LETTER VIII.

MY DEAR FRIEND,

Your letter raised me for a moment from the depths of despair; but not hearing from you yesterday or to-day (as I hoped) I have had a relapse. You say I want to get rid of her. I hope you are more right in your conjectures about her than in this about me. Oh no! believe it, I love her as I do my own soul; my very heart is wedded to her (be she what she may) and I would not hesitate a moment between her and "an angel from Heaven." I grant all you say about my self-tormenting folly: but has it been without cause? Has she not refused me again and again with a mixture of scorn and resentment, after going the utmost lengths with a man for whom she now dis-

claims all affection ; and what security can
I have for her reserve with others, who will
not be restrained by feelings of delicacy
towards her, and whom she has probably
preferred to me for their want of it ? "*She
can make no more confidences*"—these words
ring for ever in my ears, and will be my
death-watch. They can have but one meaning, be sure of it—she always expressed
herself with the exactest propriety. That
was one of the things for which I loved her
—shall I live to hate her for it ? My poor
fond heart, that brooded over her and the
remains of her affections as my only hope
of comfort upon earth, cannot brook this
new degradation. Who is there so low as
me ? Who is there besides (I ask) after the
homage I have paid her and the caresses
she has lavished on me, so vile, so abhorrent
to love, to whom such an indignity could
have happened ? When I think of this
(and I think of nothing else) it stifles me.
I am pent up in burning, fruitless desires,
which can find no vent or object. Am I
not hated, repulsed, derided by her whom

alone I love or ever did love? I cannot
stay in any place, and seek in vain for relief
from the sense of her contempt and her ingratitude. I can settle to nothing: what is
the use of all I have done? Is it not that
very circumstance (my thinking beyond my
strength, my feeling more than I need about
so many things) that has withered me up,
and made me a thing for Love to shrink
from and wonder at? Who could ever feel
that peace from the touch of her dear hand
that I have done; and is it not torn from
me for ever? My state is this, that I shall
never lie down again at night nor rise up in
the morning in peace, nor ever behold my
little boy's face with pleasure while I live—
unless I am restored to her favour. Instead
of that delicious feeling I had when she
was heavenly-kind to me, and my heart
softened and melted in its own tenderness
and her sweetness, I am now inclosed in a
dungeon of despair. The sky is marble to
my thoughts; nature is dead around me, as
hope is within me; no object can give me
one gleam of satisfaction now, nor the pros-

pect of it in time to come. I wander by
the sea-side; and the eternal ocean and
lasting despair and her face are before me.
Slighted by her, on whom my heart by its
last fibre hung, where shall I turn? I wake
with her by my side, not as my sweet bed-
fellow, but as the corpse of my love, without a heart in her bosom, cold, insensible,
or struggling from me; and the worm gnaws
me, and the sting of unrequited love, and
the canker of a hopeless, endless sorrow. I
have lost the taste of my food by feverish
anxiety; and my favourite beverage, which
used to refresh me when I got up, has no
moisture in it. Oh! cold, solitary, sepulchral breakfasts, compared with those which
I promised myself with her; or which I
made when she had been standing an hour
by my side, my guardian-angel, my wife, my
sister, my sweet friend, my Eve, my all;
and had blest me with her seraph-kisses!
Ah! what I suffer at present only shews
what I have enjoyed. But "the girl is a
good girl, if there is goodness in human
nature." I thank you for those words; and

I will fall down and worship you, if you can
prove them true : and I would not do much
less for him that proves her a demon.   She
is one or the other, that's certain ; but I fear
the worst.   Do let me know if any thing
has passed : suspense is my greatest punishment.   I am going into the country to see
if I can work a little in the three weeks I
have yet to stay here.   Write on the receipt
of this, and believe me ever your unspeakably obliged friend.

TO EDINBURGH.

——"Stony-hearted" Edinburgh! What
art thou to me? The dust of thy streets
mingles with my tears and blinds me. City
of palaces, or of tombs—a quarry, rather
than the habitation of men! Art thou like
London, that populous hive, with its sun-
burnt, well-baked, brick-built houses—its
public edifices, its theatres, its bridges, its
squares, its ladies, and its pomp, its throng
of wealth, its outstretched magnitude, and
its mighty heart that never lies still? Thy
cold grey walls reflect back the leaden melancholy of the soul. The square, hard-
edged, unyielding faces of thy inhabitants
have no sympathy to impart. What is it
to me that I look along the level line of thy
tenantless streets, and meet perhaps a law-
yer like a grasshopper chirping and skip-

ping, or the daughter of a Highland laird, haughty, fair, and freckled ? Or why should I look down your boasted Prince's-street, with the beetle-browed Castle on one side, and the Calton-hill with its proud monument at the further end, and the ridgy steep of Salisbury-Crag, cut off abruptly by Nature's boldest hand, and Arthur's-Seat overlooking all, like a lioness watching her cubs ? Or shall I turn to the far-off Pentland-hills, with Craig-Crook nestling beneath them, where lives the prince of critics and the king of men ? Or cast my eye unsated over the Frith of Forth, that from my window of an evening (as I read of AMY and her love) glitters like a broad golden mirror in the sun, and kisses the winding shores of kingly Fife ? Oh no ! But to thee, to thee I turn, North Berwick-Law, with thy blue cone rising out of summer seas ; for thou art the beacon of my banished thoughts, and dost point my way to her, who is my heart's true home. The air is too thin for me, that has not the breath of Love in it ; that is not embalmed by her sighs !

A THOUGHT.

I am not mad, but my heart is so; and raves within me, fierce and untameable, like a panther in its den, and tries to get loose to its lost mate, and fawn on her hand, and bend lowly at her feet.

ANOTHER.

Oh! thou dumb heart, lonely, sad, shut up in the prison-house of this rude form, that hast never found a fellow but for an instant, and in very mockery of thy misery, speak, find bleeding words to express thy thoughts, break thy dungeon-gloom, or die pronouncing thy Infelice's name!

ANOTHER.

Within my heart is lurking suspicion, and base fear, and shame and hate; but above all, tyrannous love sits throned, crowned with her graces, silent and in tears.

LETTER IX.

MY DEAR P——

You have been very kind to me in this business; but I fear even your indulgence for my infirmities is beginning to fail. To what a state am I reduced, and for what? For fancying a little artful vixen to be an angel and a saint, because she affected to look like one, to hide her rank thoughts and deadly purposes. Has she not murdered me under the mask of the tenderest friendship? And why? Because I have loved her with unutterable love, and sought to make her my wife. You say it is my own " outrageous conduct" that has estranged her; nay, I have been *too gentle* with her. I ask you first in candour whether the ambiguity of her behaviour with respect to me, sitting and fondling a man (circumstanced as I was) sometimes

for half a day together, and then declaring
she had no love for him beyond common regard, and professing never to marry, was not
enough to excite my suspicions, which the
different exposures from the conversations
below-stairs were not calculated to allay? I
ask you what you yourself would have felt or
done, if loving her as I did, you had heard
what I did, time after time? Did not her
mother own to one of the grossest charges
(which I shall not repeat)—and is such inde-
licacy to be reconciled with her pretended
character (that character with which I fell in
love, and to which I *made love*) without supposing her to be the greatest hypocrite in
the world? My unpardonable offence has
been that I took her at her word, and was
willing to believe her the precise little puri-
tanical person she set up for. After exciting
her wayward desires by the fondest embraces
and the purest kisses, as if she had been
"made my wedded wife yestreen," or was to
become so to-morrow (for that was always
my feeling with respect to her)—I did not
proceed to gratify them, or to follow up my

advantage by any action which should declare, "I think you a common adventurer,
and will see whether you are so or not!"
Yet any one but a credulous fool like me
would have made the experiment, with whatever violence to himself, as a matter of life
and death ; for I had every reason to distrust
appearances. Her conduct has been of a
piece from the beginning. In the midst of
her closest and falsest endearments, she has
always (with one or two exceptions) disclaimed the natural inference to be drawn
from them, and made a verbal reservation,
by which she might lead me on in a Fool's
Paradise, and make me the tool of her levity,
her avarice, and her love of intrigue as long
as she liked, and dismiss me whenever it
suited her. This, you see, she has done,
because my intentions grew serious, and if
complied with, would deprive her of *the plea-
sures of a single life !* Offer marriage to this
"tradesman's daughter, who has as nice a
sense of honour as any one can have ;" and
like Lady Bellaston in *Tom Jones* she *cuts*
you immediately in a fit of abhorrence and

alarm. Yet she seemed to be of a different mind formerly, when struggling from me in the height of our first intimacy, she exclaimed—" However I might agree to my own ruin, I never will consent to bring disgrace upon my family !" That I should have spared the traitress after expressions like this, astonishes me when I look back upon it. Yet if it were all to do over again, I know I should act just the same part. Such is her power over me ! I cannot run the least risk of offending her—I love her so. When I look in her face, I cannot doubt her truth ! Wretched being that I am ! I have thrown away my heart and soul upon an unfeeling girl ! and my life (that might have been so happy, had she been what I thought her) will soon follow either voluntarily, or by the force of grief, remorse, and disappointment. I cannot get rid of the reflection for an instant, nor even seek relief from its galling pressure. Ah ! what a heart she has lost ! All the love and affection of my whole life were centred in her, who alone, I thought, of all women had

found out my true character, and knew how
to value my tenderness. Alas! alas! that
this, the only hope, joy, or comfort I ever
had, should turn to a mockery, and hang like
an ugly film over the remainder of my
days!—I was at Roslin Castle yesterday.
It lies low in a rude, but sheltered valley,
hid from the vulgar gaze, and powerfully
reminds one of the old song. The straggling fragments of the russet ruins, suspend-
ed smiling and graceful in the air as if they
would linger out another century to please
the curious beholder, the green larch-trees
trembling between with the blue sky and
white silver clouds, the wild mountain plants
starting out here and there, the date of the
year on an old low door-way, but still more,
the beds of flowers in orderly decay, that
seem to have no hand to tend them, but
keep up a sort of traditional remembrance
of civilization in former ages, present
altogether a delightful and amiable subject
for contemplation. The exquisite beauty of
the scene, with the thought of what I should
feel, should I ever be restored to her, and

have to lead her through such places as my
adored, my angel-wife, almost drove me
beside myself. For this picture, this ecstatic
vision, what have I of late instead as the
image of the reality? Demoniacal posses-
sions. I see the young witch seated in
another's lap, twining her serpent arms
round him, her eye glancing and her cheeks
on fire—why does not the hideous thought
choke me? Or why do I not go and find
out the truth at once? The moonlight
streams over the silver waters: the bark is
in the bay that might waft me to her, almost
with a wish. The mountain-breeze sighs
out her name: old ocean with a world of
tears murmurs back my woes! Does not
my heart yearn to be with her; and shall I
not follow its bidding? No, I must wait
till I am free; and then I will take my
Freedom (a glad prize) and lay it at her
feet and tell her my proud love of her that
would not brook a rival in her dishonour,
and that would have her all or none, and
gain her or lose myself for ever!—

You see by this letter the way I am in,

and I hope you will excuse it as the picture of a half-disordered mind. The least respite from my uneasiness (such as I had yesterday) only brings the contrary reflection back upon me, like a flood; and by letting me see the happiness I have lost, makes me feel, by contrast, more acutely what I am doomed to bear.

LETTER X.

DEAR FRIEND,

Here I am at St. Bees once more, amid the scenes which I greeted in their barrenness in winter; but which have now put on their full green attire that shows luxuriant to the eye, but speaks a tale of sadness to this heart widowed of its last, its dearest, its only hope! Oh! lovely Bees-Inn! here I composed a volume of law-cases, here I wrote my enamoured follies to her, thinking her human, and that "all below was not the fiend's"—here I got two cold, sullen answers from the little witch, and here I was———— and I was damned. I thought the revisiting the old haunts would have soothed me for a time, but it only brings back the sense of what I have suffered for her and of her unkindness the more strongly, till I cannot en-

dure the recollection. I eye the Heavens in
dumb despair, or vent my sorrows in the
desart air. "To the winds, to the waves, to
the rocks I complain"—you may suppose
with what effect! I fear I shall be obliged
to return. I am tossed about (backwards
and forwards) by my passion, so as to become ridiculous. I can now understand
how it is that mad people never remain in
the same place—they are moving on for ever,
from themselves!

Do you know, you would have been delighted with the effect of the Northern twilight on this romantic country as I rode
along last night? The hills and groves and
herds of cattle were seen reposing in the
grey dawn of midnight, as in a moonlight
without shadow. The whole wide canopy
of Heaven shed its reflex light upon them,
like a pure crystal mirror. No sharp points,
no pretty details, no hard contrasts—every
object was seen softened yet distinct, in its
simple outline and natural tones, trans-
parent with an inward light, breathing its
own mild lustre. The landscape altogether

was like an airy piece of mosaic-work, or
like one of Poussin's broad massy land-
scapes or Titian's lovely pastoral scenes.   Is
it not so, that poets see nature, veiled to the
sight, but revealed to the soul in visionary
grace and grandeur!   I confess the sight
touched me ; and might have removed all
sadness except mine.   So (I thought) the
light of her celestial face once shone into
my soul, and wrapt me in a heavenly trance.
The sense I have of beauty raises me for a
moment above myself, but depresses me the
more afterwards, when I recollect how it is
thrown away in vain admiration, and that it
only makes me more susceptible of pain
from the mortifications I meet with.   Would
I had never seen her!   I might then not indeed have been happy, but at least I might
have passed my life in peace, and have sunk
into forgetfulness without a pang.—The
noble scenery in this country mixes with my
passion, and refines, but does not relieve it.
I was at Stirling Castle not long ago.   It
gave me no pleasure.   The declivity seemed
to me abrupt, not sublime ; for in truth I did

not shrink back from it with terror. The
weather-beaten towers were stiff and formal:
the air was damp and chill: the river winded
its dull, slimy way like a snake along the
marshy grounds: and the dim misty tops of
Ben Leddi, and the lovely Highlands (woven
fantastically of thin air) mocked my embraces
and tempted my longing eyes like her, the
sole queen and mistress of my thoughts! I
never found my contemplations on this subject so subtilised and at the same time so
desponding as on that occasion. I wept
myself almost blind, and I gazed at the broad
golden sun-set through my tears that fell in
showers. As I trod the green mountain turf,
oh! how I wished to be laid beneath it—in
one grave with her—that I might sleep with
her in that cold bed, my hand in hers, and
my heart for ever still—while worms should
taste her sweet body, that I had never tasted!
There was a time when I could bear solitude;
but it is too much for me at present. Now
I am no sooner left to myself than I am
lost in infinite space, and look round me in
vain for support or comfort. She was my

stay, my hope : without her hand to cling to,
I stagger like an infant on the edge of a precipice. The universe without her is one
wide, hollow abyss, in which my harassed
thoughts can find no resting-place. I must
break off here ; for the *hysterica passio* comes
upon me, and threatens to unhinge my
reason.

LETTER XI.

MY DEAR AND GOOD FRIEND,

I am afraid I trouble you with my querulous epistles, but this is probably the last.
To-morrow or the next day decides my fate
with respect to the divorce, when I expect
to be a free man. In vain! Was is not for
her and to lay my freedom at her feet, that
I consented to this step which has cost me
infinite perplexity, and now to be discarded
for the first pretender that came in her way!
If so, I hardly think I can survive it. You
who have been a favourite with women, do
not know what it is to be deprived of one's
only hope, and to have it turned to shame
and disappointment. There is nothing in
the world left that can afford me one drop of
comfort—*this* I feel more and more. Every
thing is to me a mockery of pleasure, like

her love. The breeze does not cool me: the
blue sky does not cheer me. I gaze only on
her face averted from me—alas! the only
face that ever was turned fondly to me!
And why am I thus treated? Because I
wanted her to be mine for ever in love or
friendship, and did not push my gross familiarities as far as I might. "Why can you
not go on as we have done, and say nothing about the word, *forever ?*" Was it not
plain from this that she even then medi-
tated an escape from me to some less sentimental lover? "Do you allow any one
else to do so ?" I said to her once, as I was
toying with her. "No, not now!" was her
answer; that is, because there was nobody
else in the house to take freedoms with her.
I was very well as a stopgap, but I was to be
nothing more. While the coast was clear, I
had it all my own way: but the instance
C—— came, she flung herself at his head
in the most bare-faced way, ran breathless
up stairs before him, blushed when his foot
was heard, watched for him in the passage,
and was sure to be in close conference with

him when he went down again. It was then
my mad proceedings commenced. No wonder. Had I not reason to be jealous of
every appearance of familiarity with others,
knowing how easy she had been with me at
first, and that she only grew shy when I did
not take farther liberties? What has her
character to rest upon but her attachment
to me, which she now denies, not modestly,
but impudently? Will you yourself say that
if she had all along no particular regard for
me, she will not do as much or more with
other more likely men? "She has had,"
she says, "enough of my conversation," so
it could not be that! Ah! my friend, it was
not to be supposed I should ever meet even
with the outward demonstrations of regard
from any woman but a common trader in the
endearments of love! I have tasted the
sweets of the well practised illusion, and
now feel the bitterness of knowing what a
bliss I am deprived of, and must ever be deprived of. Intolerable conviction! Yet I
might, I believe, have won her by other
methods; but some demon held my hand.

How indeed could I offer her the least insult
when I worshipped her very footsteps ; and
even now pay her divine honours from my
inmost heart, whenever I think of her, abased
and brutalised as I have been by that Circean
cup of kisses, of enchantments, of which I
have drunk ! I am choked, withered, dried
up with chagrin, remorse, despair, from
which I have not a moment's respite, day or
night. I have always some horrid dream
about her, and wake wondering what is the
matter that " she is no longer the same to
me as ever ?" I thought at least we should
always remain dear friends, if nothing more
—did she not talk of coming to live with me
only the day before I left her in the winter ?
But " she's gone, I am abused, and my revenge must be to *love* her !"—Yet she knows
that one line, one word would save me, the
cruel, heartless destroyer ! I see nothing
for it but madness, unless Friday brings a
change, or unless she is willing to let me go
back. You must know I wrote to her to that
purpose, but it was a very quiet, sober letter,
begging pardon, and professing reform for

the future, and all that.   What effect it will
have, I know not.   I was forced to get out
of the way of her answer, till Friday came.

Ever your's.

TO S. L.

MY DEAR MISS L——,

Evil to them that evil think, is an old saying; and I have found it a true one. I have ruined myself by my unjust suspicions of you. Your sweet friendship was the balm of my life; and I have lost it, I fear for ever, by one fault and folly after another. What would I give to be restored to the place in your esteem, which, you assured me, I held only a few months ago! Yet I was not contented, but did all I could to torment myself and harass you by endless doubts and jealousy. Can you not forget and forgive the past, and judge of me by my conduct in future? Can you not take all my follies in the lump, and say like a good, generous girl, "Well, I'll think no more of them ?" In a word, may I come back, and try to behave better? A line to say so would be an additional favour to so many already received by

Your obliged friend,

And sincere well-wisher.

LETTER XII. TO C. P——.

I have no answer from her. I'm mad. I wish you to call on M—— in confidence, to say I intend to make her an offer of my hand, and that I will write to her father to that effect the instant I am free, and ask him whether he thinks it will be to any purpose, and what he would advise me to do.

UNALTERED LOVE.

"Love is not love that alteration finds:
  Oh no! it is an ever-fixed mark,
  That looks on tempests and is never shaken."

SHALL I not love her for herself alone,
in spite of fickleness and folly? To love
her for her regard to me, is not to love her,
but myself. She has robbed me of herself:
shall she also rob me of my love of her?
Did I not live on her smile? Is it less
sweet because it is withdrawn from me?
Did I not adore her every grace? Does she
bend less enchantingly, because she has
turned from me to another? Is my love
then in the power of fortune, or of her caprice? No, I will have it lasting as it is
pure; and I will make a Goddess of her,
and build a temple to her in my heart, and
worship her on indestructible altars, and

raise statues to her: and my homage shall
be unblemished as her unrivalled symmetry
of form; and when that fails, the memory
of it shall survive; and my bosom shall be
proof to scorn, as her's has been to pity;
and I will pursue her with an unrelenting
love, and sue to be her slave, and tend her
steps without notice and without reward;
and serve her living, and mourn for her
when dead. And thus my love will have
shewn itself superior to her hate; and I
shall triumph and then die. This is my idea
of the only true and heroic love! Such is
mine for her.

PERFECT LOVE.

PERFECT love has this advantage in it, that it leaves the possessor of it nothing farther to desire. There is one object (at least) in which the soul finds absolute content, for which it seeks to live, or dares to die. The heart has as it were filled up the moulds of the imagination. The truth of passion keeps pace with and outvies the extravagance of mere language. There are no words so fine, no flattery so soft, that there is not a sentiment beyond them, that it is impossible to express, at the bottom of the heart where true love is. What idle sounds the common phrases, *adorable creature, angel, divinity,* are! What a proud reflection it is to have a feeling answering to all these, rooted in the breast, unalterable, unutterable, to which all other feelings are light and vain! Perfect love reposes on the object of its choice, like the halcyon on the wave; and the air of heaven is around it.

FROM C. P. ESQ.

London, July 4th, 1822.

I have seen M——! Now, my dear H—,
let me entreat and adjure you to take what
I have to tell you, *for what it is worth*—
neither for less, nor more. In the first
place, I have learned nothing decisive from
him. This, as you will at once see, is, as
far as it goes, good. I am either to hear
from him, or see him again in a day or two;
but I thought you would like to know what
passed inconclusive as it was—so I write
without delay, and in great haste to save a
post. I found him frank, and even friendly
in his manner to me, and in his views re-
specting you. I think that he is sincerely
sorry for your situation; and he feels that
the person who has placed you in that situ-

ation is not much less awkwardly situated herself; and he professes that he would willingly do what he can for the good of both. But he sees great difficulties attending the affair—which he frankly professes to consider as an altogether unfortunate one. With respect to the marriage, he seems to see the most formidable objections to it, on both sides; but yet he by no means decidedly says that it cannot, or that it ought not to take place. These, mind you, are his own feelings on the subject: but the most important point I learn from him is this, that he is not prepared to use his influence either way—that the rest of the family are of the same way of feeling; and that, in fact, the thing must and does entirely rest with herself. To learn this was, as you see, gaining a great point.—When I then endeavoured to ascertain whether he knew any thing decisive as to what are her views on the subject, I found that he did not. He has an opinion on the subject, and he didn't scruple to tell me what it was; but he has no positive knowledge. In short,

he believes, from what he learns from herself (and he had purposely seen her on
the subject, in consequence of my application to him) that she is at present indis-
posed to the marriage; but he is not
prepared to say positively that she will not
consent to it. Now all this, coming from
him in the most frank and unaffected
manner, and without any appearance of
cant, caution, or reserve, I take to be most
important as it respects your views, whatever
they may be; and certainly much more
favorable to them (I confess it) than I was
prepared to expect, supposing them to
remain as they were. In fact, as I said
before, the affair rests entirely with herself.
They are none of them disposed either to
further the marriage, or throw any insur-
mountable obstacles in the way of it; and
what is more important than all, they are
evidently by no means *certain* that SHE may
not, at some future period, consent to it;
or they would, for her sake as well as their
own, let you know as much flatly, and put
an end to the affair at once.

Seeing in how frank and straitforward a manner he received what I had to say to him, and replied to it, I proceeded to ask him what were *his* views, and what were likely to be *her's* (in case she did not consent) as to whether you should return to live in the house ;—but I added, without waiting for his answer, that if she intended to persist in treating you as she had done for some time past, it would be worse than madness for you to think of returning. I added that, in case you did return, all you would expect from her would be that she would treat you with civility and kindness— that she would continue to evince that friendly feeling towards you, that she had done for a great length of time, &c. To this, he said, he could really give no decisive reply, but that he should be most happy if, by any intervention of his, he could conduce to your comfort ; but he seemed to think that for you to return on any express understanding that she should behave to you in any particular manner, would be to place her in a most awkward situation. He

went somewhat at length into this point,
and talked very reasonably about it; the
result however was that he would not throw
any obstacles in the way of your return, or
of her treating you as a friend, &c. nor did
it appear that he believed she would refuse
to do so. And, finally, we parted on the
understanding that he would see them on
the subject, and ascertain what could be
done for the comfort of all parties : though
he was of opinion that if you could make
up your mind to break off the acquaintance
altogether, it would be the best plan of all.
I am to hear from him again in a day or two.
—Well, what do you say to all this ? Can
you turn it to any thing but good—compar-
ative good ? If you would know what *I* say
to it, it is this :—She is still to be won by
wise and prudent conduct on your part ;—
she was always to have been won by such ;—
and if she is lost, it has been (not, as you
sometimes suppose, because you have not
carried that unwise, may I not say *unworthy ?*
conduct still farther, but) because you gave
way to it at all. Of course I use the terms

" wise " and " prudent " with reference to
your object.   Whether the pursuit of that
object is wise, only yourself can judge.   I
say she has all along been to be won, and
she still is to be won ; and all that stands in
the way of your views at this moment is
your past conduct.   They are all of them,
every soul, frightened at you ; they have *seen*
enough of you to make them so ; and they
have doubtless heard ten times more than
they have seen, or than any one else has
seen. They are all of them, including M——
(and particularly she herself) frightened out
of their wits, as to what might be your
treatment of her if she were your's ; and
they dare not trust you—they will not trust
you, at present.   I do not say that they will
trust you or rather that *she* will, for it all
depends on her, when you have gone through
a probation, but I am sure that she will not
trust you till you have.   You will, I hope,
not be angry with me when I say that she
would be a fool if she did.   If she were to
accept you at present, and without knowing
more of you, even *I* should begin to suspect

that she had an unworthy motive for doing it
Let me not forget to mention what is perhaps
as important a point as any, as it regards the
marriage. I of course stated to M—— that
when you are free, you are prepared to make
her a formal offer of your hand; but I begged
him, if he was certain that such an offer
would be refused, to tell me so plainly at
once, that I might endeavour, in that case,
to dissuade you from subjecting yourself to
the pain of such a refusal. *He would not
tell me that he was certain.* He said his
opinion was that she would not accept your
offer, but still he seemed to think that there
would be no harm in making it!—One word
more, and a very important one. He once,
and without my referring in the slightest
manner to that part of the subject, spoke of
her as a *good girl*, and *likely to make any man
an excellent wife!* Do you think if she were
a bad girl (and if she were, he must know
her to be so) he would have dared to do this,
under these circumstances ?—And once, in
speaking of *his* not being a fit person to set
his face against "marrying for love," he

added "I did so myself, and out of that
house; and I have had reason to rejoice at
it ever since." And mind (for I anticipate
your cursed suspicions) I'm certain, at least,
if manner can entitle one to be certain of
any thing, that he said all this spontaneously,
and without any understood motive; and I'm
certain, too, that he knows you to be a
person it would not do to play any tricks of
this kind with. I believe—(and all this
would never have entered my thoughts, but
that I know it will enter your's) I believe
that even if they thought (as you have sometimes supposed they do) that she needs
whitewashing, or making an honest woman
of, *you* would be the last person they would
think of using for such a purpose, for they
know (as well as I do) that you couldn't fail
to find out the trick in a month, and would
turn her into the street the next moment,
though she were twenty times your wife—
and that, as to the consequences of doing
so, you would laugh at them, even if you
cou'dn't escape from them.—I shall lose the
post if I say more.

Believe me, Ever truly your friend,
C.P.

LETTER XIII.

MY DEAR P——,

You have saved my life. If I do not keep friends with her now, I deserve to be hanged, drawn, and quartered. She is an angel from Heaven, and you cannot pretend I ever said a word to the contrary! The little rogue must have liked me from the first, or she never could have stood all these hurricanes without slipping her cable. What could she find in me? "I have mistook my person all this while," &c. Do you know I saw a picture, the very pattern of her, the other day, at Dalkeith Palace (Hope finding Fortune in the Sea) just before this blessed news came, and the resemblance drove me almost out of my senses. Such delicacy, such fulness, such perfect softness, such buoyancy,

such grace! If it is not the very image of
her, I am no judge.—You have the face to
doubt my making the best husband in the
world: you might as well doubt it if I was
married to one of the Houris of Paradise.
She is a saint, an angel, a love. If she
deceives me again, she kills me. But I will
have such a kiss when I get back, as shall
last me twenty years. May God bless her
for not utterly disowning and destroying me!
What an exquisite little creature it is, and
how she holds out to the last in her system
of consistent contradictions! Since I wrote
to you about making a formal proposal, I
have had her face constantly before me,
looking so like some faultless marble statue,
as cold, as fixed and graceful as ever statue
did; the expression (nothing was ever like
that!) seemed to say—" I wish I could love
you better than I do, but still I will be your's."
No, I'll never believe again that she will not
be mine; for I think she was made on purpose for me. If there's any one else that
understands that turn of her head as I do,
I'll give her up without scruple. I have

made up my mind to this, never to dream of
another woman, while she even thinks it
worth her while to *refuse to have me*. You
see I am not hard to please, after all.   Did
M—— know of the intimacy that had sub-
sisted between us ?   Or did you hint at it ?
I think it would be a *clencher*, if he did.
How ought I to behave when I go back ?
Advise a fool, who had nearly lost a Goddess
by his folly. The thing was, I could not think
it possible she should ever like *me*.   Her
taste is singular, but not the worse for that.
I'd rather have her love, or liking (call it
what you will) than empires.   I deserve to
call her mine ; for nothing else *can* atone for
what I've gone through for her.   I hope your
next letter will not reverse all, and then I
shall be happy till I see her—one of the blest
when I do see her, if she looks like my own
beautiful love.   I may perhaps write a line
when I come to my right wits.—Farewel at
present, and thank you a thousand times
for what you have done for your poor
friend.

P.S. I like what M—— said about her sister, much. There are good people in the world : I begin to see it, and believe it.

LETTER THE LAST.

DEAR P——,

To-morrow is the decisive day that makes me or mars me. I will let you know the result by a line added to this. Yet what signifies it, since either way I have little hope there, "whence alone my hope cometh!" You must know I am strangely in the dumps at this present writing. My reception with her is doubtful, and my fate is then certain. The hearing of your happiness has, I own, made me thoughtful. It is just what I proposed to her to do—to have crossed the Alps with me, to sail on sunny seas, to bask in Italian skies, to have visited Vevai and the rocks of Meillerie, and to have repeated to her on the spot the story of Julia and St. Preux, and to have shewn her all that my

heart had stored up for her—but on my forehead alone is written—REJECTED! Yet I
too could have adored as fervently, and
loved as tenderly as others, had I been permitted. You are going abroad, you say,
happy in making happy. Where shall I be?
In the grave, I hope, or else in her arms.
To me, alas! there is no sweetness out of
her sight, and that sweetness has turned to
bitterness, I fear; that gentleness to sullen
scorn! Still I hope for the best. If she
will but *have* me, I'll make her *love* me: and
I think her not giving a positive answer
looks like it, and also shews that there is no
one else. Her holding out to the last also,
I think, proves that she was never to have
been gained but with honour. She's a strange,
almost an inscrutable girl: but if I once win
her consent, I shall kill her with kindness.
—Will you let me have a sight of *somebody* before you go? I should be most proud. I was
in hopes to have got away by the Steam-boat
to-morrow, but owing to the business not
coming on till then, I cannot; and may not
be in town for another week, unless I come

by the Mail, which I am strongly tempted to do. In the latter case I shall be *there*, and visible on Saturday evening. Will you look in and see, about eight o'clock? I wish much to see you and her and J. H. and my little boy once more; and then, if she is not what she once was to me, I care not if I die that instant. I will conclude here till to-morrow, as I am getting into my old melancholy.—

It is all over, and I am my own man, and your's ever—

LIBER AMORIS.

PART III.

ADDRESSED TO J. S. K——.

MY DEAR K——,

It is all over, and I know my fate. I told
you I would send you word, if any thing
decisive happened; but an impenetrable
mystery hung over the affair till lately. It
is at last (by the merest accident in the
world) dissipated; and I keep my promise,
both for your satisfaction, and for the ease
of my own mind.

You remember the morning when I said
"I will go and repose my sorrows at the foot
of Ben Lomond"—and when from Dumbar-
ton-bridge its giant-shadow, clad in air and
sunshine, appeared in view. We had a
pleasant day's walk. We passed Smollet's
monument on the road (somehow these
poets touch one in reflection more than most

military heroes)—talked of old times; you
repeated Logan's beautiful verses to the
cuckoo,* which I wanted to compare with
Wordsworth's, but my courage failed me;
you then told me some passages of an early
attachment which was suddenly broken off;
we considered together which was the most
to be pitied, a disappointment in love where
the attachment was mutual or one where
there has been no return, and we both agreed,
I think, that the former was best to be endured, and that to have the consciousness of

> * " Sweet bird, thy bower is ever green,
>   Thy sky is ever clear;
>   Thou hast no sorrow in thy song,
>   No winter in thy year."

So they begin. It was the month of May; the cuckoo
sang shrouded in some woody copse; the showers
fell between whiles; my friend repeated the lines with
native enthusiasm in a clear manly voice, still resonant
of youth and hope. Mr. Wordsworth will excuse
me, if in these circumstances I declined entering the
field with his profounder metaphysical strain, and kept
my preference to myself.

it a companion for life was the least evil of
the two, as there was a secret sweetness that
took off the bitterness and the sting of regret,
and " the memory of what once had been "
atoned, in some measure, and at intervals, for
what " never more could be."   In the other
case, there was nothing to look back to with
tender satisfaction, no redeeming trait, not
even a possibility of turning it to good.   It
left behind it not cherished sighs, but stifled
pangs.   The galling sense of it did not bring
moisture into the eyes, but dried up the
heart ever after.   One had been my fate, the
other had been yours !—

You startled me every now and then from
my reverie by the robust voice, in which you
asked the country people (by no means pro-
digal of their answers)—" If there was any
trout-fishing in those streams ?"—and our
dinner at Luss set us up for the rest of our
day's march.   The sky now became over-
cast ; but this, I think, added to the effect
of the scene.   The road to Tarbet is superb.
It is on the very verge of the lake—hard
level, rocky, with low stone-bridges con-

stantly flung across it, and fringed with birch
trees, just then budding into spring, behind
which, as through a slight veil, you saw the
huge shadowy form of Ben Lomond.   It lifts
its enormous but graceful bulk direct from the
edge of the water without any projecting
lowlands, and has in this respect much the
advantage of Skiddaw.   Loch Lomond comes
upon you by degrees as you advance, un-
folding and then withdrawing its conscious
beauties like an accomplished coquet.   You
are struck with the point of a rock, the arch
of a bridge, the Highland huts (like the first
rude habitations of men) dug out of the soil,
built of turf, and covered with brown heather,
a sheep-cote, some straggling cattle feeding
half-way down a precipice ; but as you advance farther on, the view expands into the
perfection of lake scenery.   It is nothing (or
your eye is caught by nothing) but water,
earth, and sky.   Ben Lomond waves to the
right, in its simple majesty, cloud-capt or
bare, and descending to a point at the head
of the lake, shews the Trossacs beyond,
tumbling about their blue ridges like woods

waving ; to the left is the Cobler, whose top
is like a castle shattered in pieces and nod-
ding to its ruin ; and at your side rise the
shapes of round pastoral hills, green, fleeced
with herds, and retiring into mountainous
bays and upland valleys, where solitude and
peace might make their lasting home, if
peace were to be found in solitude ! That it
was not always so, I was a sufficient proof ;
for there was one image that alone haunted
me in the midst of all this sublimity and
beauty, and turned it to a mockery and a
dream !

The snow on the mountain would not let
us ascend ; and being weary of waiting and
of being visited by the guide every two
hours to let us know that the weather would
not do, we returned, you homewards, and I
to London—

"Italiam, Italiam !"

You know the anxious expectations with
which I set out :—now hear the result.—

As the vessel sailed up the Thames, the
air thickened with the consciousness of

being near her, and I "heaved her name
pantingly forth." As I approached the
house, I could not help thinking of the
lines—

> " How near am I to happiness,
> That earth exceeds not ! Not another like it.
> The treasures of the deep are not so precious
> As are the concealed comforts of a man
> Lock'd up in woman's love. I scent the air
> Of blessings when I come but near the house.
> What a delicious breath true love sends forth !
> The violet-beds not sweeter. Now for a welcome
> Able to draw men's envies upon man :
> A kiss now that will hang upon my lip,
> As sweet as morning dew upon a rose,
> And full as long ! "

I saw her, but I saw at the first glance that
there was something amiss. It was with
much difficulty and after several pressing
intreaties that she was prevailed on to come
up into the room ; and when she did, she
stood at the door, cold, distant, averse ; and
when at length she was persuaded by my
repeated remonstrances to come and take
my hand, and I offered to touch her lips,
she turned her head and shrunk from my

embraces, as if quite alienated or mortally offended. I asked what it could mean? What had I done in her absence to have incurred her displeasure? Why had she not written to me? I could get only short, sullen, disconnected answers, as if there was something labouring in her mind which she either could not or would not impart. I hardly knew how to bear this first reception after so long an absence, and so different from the one my sentiments towards her merited; but I thought it possible it might be prudery (as I had returned without having actually accomplished what I went about) or that she had taken offence at something in my letters. She saw how much I was hurt. I asked her, "If she was altered since I went away?" — "No." "If there was any one else who had been so fortunate as to gain her favourable opinion?"—"No, there was no one else." "What was it then? Was it any thing in my letters? Or had I displeased her by letting Mr. P—— know she wrote to me?"—"No, not at all; but she did not apprehend my last letter required any an-

swer, or she would have replied to it." All
this appeared to me very unsatisfactory and
evasive; but I could get no more from her,
and was obliged to let her go with a heavy,
foreboding heart. I however found that
C—— was gone, and no one else had been
there, of whom I had cause to be jealous.
—"Should I see her on the morrow?"—
"She believed so, but she could not promise." The next morning she did not
appear with the breakfast as usual. At this
I grew somewhat uneasy. The little Buonaparte, however, was placed in its old position
on the mantle-piece, which I considered as
a sort of recognition of old times. I saw her
once or twice casually; nothing particular
happened till the next day, which was Sunday. I took occasion to go into the parlour
for the newspaper, which she gave me with
a gracious smile, and seemed tolerably frank
and cordial. This of course acted as a spell
upon me. I walked out with my little boy,
intending to go and dine out at one or two
places, but I found that I still contrived to
bend my steps towards her, and I went back

to take tea at home.   While we were out, I
talked to William about Sarah, saying that
she too was unhappy, and asking him to
make it up with her.   He said, if she was
unhappy, he would not bear her malice any
more.   When she came up with the tea-
things, I said to her, "William has something
to say to you—I believe he wants to be
friends."   On which he said in his abrupt,
hearty manner, "Sarah, I'm sorry if I've
ever said any thing to vex you"—so they
shook hands, and she said, smiling affably—
"*Then* I'll think no more of it!"   I added
—"I see you've brought me back my little
Buonaparte"—She answered with tremulous
softness—"I told you I'd keep it safe for
you!"—as if her pride and pleasure in doing
so had been equal, and she had, as it were,
thought of nothing during my absence but
how to greet me with this proof of her
fidelity on my return.   I cannot describe her
manner.   Her words are few and simple ;
but you can have no idea of the exquisite,
unstudied, irresistible graces with which she
accompanies them, unless you can suppose

a Greek statue to smile, move, and speak.
Those lines in Tibullus seem to have been
written on purpose for her—

> Quicquid agit, quoquo vestigià vertit,
> Componuit furtim, subsequiturque decor.

Or what do you think of those in a modern
play, which might actually have been composed with an eye to this little trifler—

> —— " See with what a waving air she goes
> Along the corridor. How like a fawn!
> Yet statelier. No sound (however soft)
> Nor gentlest echo telleth when she treads,
> But every motion of her shape doth seem
> Hallowed by silence. So did Hebe grow
> Among the Gods a paragon! Away, I'm grown
> The very fool of Love! "

The truth is, I never saw any thing like her,
nor I never shall again. How then do I
console myself for the loss of her? Shall I
tell you, but you will not mention it again?
I am foolish enough to believe that she and
I, in spite of every thing, shall be sitting
together over a sea-coal fire, a comfortable

good old couple, twenty years hence! But
to my narrative.—

I was delighted with the alteration in her
manner, and said, referring to the bust—
"You know it is not mine, but your's; I
gave it you; nay, I have given you all—my
heart, and whatever I possess, is your's!"
She seemed good-humouredly to decline this
carte blanche offer, and waved, like a thing of
enchantment, out of the room.   False calm!
—Deceitful smiles!—Short interval of peace,
followed by lasting woe!   I sought an
interview with her that same evening. I
could not get her to come any farther
than the door. "She was busy—she could
hear what I had to say there." "Why
do you seem to avoid me as you do? Not
one five minutes' conversation, for the sake
of old acquaintance? Well, then, for the
sake of *the little image!*" The appeal seemed
to have lost its efficacy; the charm was
broken; she remained immoveable. "Well,
then, I must come to you, if you will not
run away." I went and sat down in a chair
near the door, and took her hand, and talked

to her for three quarters of an hour; and she listened patiently, thoughtfully, and seemed a good deal affected by what I said. I told her how much I had felt, how much I had suffered for her in my absence, and how much I had been hurt by her sudden silence, for which I knew not how to account. I could have done nothing to offend her while I was away; and my letters were, I hoped, tender and respectful. I had had but one thought ever present with me; her image never quitted my side, alone or in company, to delight or distract me. Without her I could have no peace, nor ever should again, unless she would behave to me as she had done formerly. There was no abatement of my regard to her; why was she so changed? I said to her, "Ah! Sarah, when I think that it is only a year ago that you were every thing to me I could wish, and that now you seem lost to me for ever, the month of May (the name of which ought to be a signal for joy and hope) strikes chill to my heart.— How different is this meeting from that delicious parting, when you seemed never

weary of repeating the proofs of your regard
and tenderness, and it was with difficulty we
tore ourselves asunder at last! I am ten
thousand times fonder of you than I was
then, and ten thousand times more unhappy."
"You have no reason to be so; my feelings
towards you are the same as they ever were."
I told her "She was my all of hope or
comfort: my passion for her grew stronger
every time I saw her." She answered,
"She was sorry for it; for *that* she never
could return." I said something about
looking ill: she said in her pretty, mincing,
emphatic way, "I despise looks!" So,
thought I, it is not that; and she says
there's no one else: it must be some strange
air she gives herself, in consequence of the
approaching change in my circumstances.
She has been probably advised not to give
up till all is fairly over, and then she will be
my own sweet girl again. All this time she
was standing just outside the door, my hand
in hers (would that they could have grown
together!) she was dressed in a loose
morning-gown, her hair curled beautifully;

she stood with her profile to me, and looked
down the whole time. No expression was
ever more soft or perfect. Her whole
attitude, her whole form, was dignity and
bewitching grace. I said to her, "You look
like a queen, my love, adorned with your
own graces!" I grew idolatrous, and would
have kneeled to her. She made a movement,
as if she was displeased. I tried to draw
her towards me. She wouldn't. I then got
up, and offered to kiss her at parting. I
found she obstinately refused. This stung
me to the quick. It was the first time in her
life she had ever done so. There must be
some new bar between us to produce these
continued denials ; and she had not even
esteem enough left to tell me so. I followed
her half-way down-stairs, but to no purpose,
and returned into my room, confirmed in my
most dreadful surmises. I could bear it no
longer. I gave way to all the fury of disappointed hope and jealous passion. I was
made the dupe of trick and cunning, killed
with cold, sullen scorn ; and, after all the
agony I had suffered, could obtain no

explanation why I was subjected to it.　I
was still to be tantalized, tortured, made the
cruel sport of one, for whom I would have
sacrificed all.　I tore the locket which
contained her hair (and which I used to
wear continually in my bosom, as the precious
token of her dear regard) from my neck,
and trampled it in pieces.　I then dashed
the little Buonaparte on the ground, and
stamped upon it, as one of her instruments
of mockery.　I could not stay in the room ;
I could not leave it ; my rage, my despair
were uncontroulable.　I shrieked curses on
her name, and on her false love ; and the
scream I uttered (so pitiful and so piercing
was it, that the sound of it terrified me)
instantly brought the whole house, father,
mother, lodgers and all, into the room.
They thought I was destroying her and
myself.　I had gone into the bed-room,
merely to hide away from myself, and as I
came out of it, raging-mad with the new
sense of present shame and lasting misery,
Mrs. F—— said, "She's in there !　He has
got her in there !" thinking the cries had

proceeded from her, and that I had been offering her violence. "Oh! no," I said, "She's in no danger from me; I am not the person;" and tried to burst from this scene of degradation. The mother endeavoured to stop me, and said, "For God's sake, don't go out, Mr. ———! for God's sake, don't!" Her father, who was not, I believe, in the secret, and was therefore justly scandalised at such outrageous conduct, said angrily, "Let him go! Why should he stay?" I however sprang down stairs, and as they called out to me, "What is it?—What has she done to you?" I answered, "She has murdered me!—She has destroyed me for ever!—She has doomed my soul to perdition!" I rushed out of the house, thinking to quit it forever; but I was no sooner in the street, than the desolation and the darkness became greater, more intolerable; and the eddying violence of my passion drove me back to the source, from whence it sprung. This unexpected explosion, with the conjectures to which it would give rise, could not be very agreeable to the *precieuse*

or her family: and when I went back, the
father was waiting at the door, as if antici-
pating this sudden turn of my feelings, with
no friendly aspect. I said, " I have to beg
pardon, Sir; but my mad fit is over, and I
wish to say a few words to you in private."
He seemed to hesitate, but some uneasy
forebodings on his own account, probably,
prevailed over his resentment ; or, perhaps
(as philosophers have a desire to know the
cause of thunder) it was a natural curiosity
to know what circumstances of provocation
had given rise to such an extraordinary scene
of confusion. When we reached my room,
I requested him to be seated. I said, " It is
true, Sir, I have lost my peace of mind
forever, but at present I am quite calm and
collected, and I wish to explain to you why
I have behaved in so extravagant a way, and
to ask for your advice and intercession."
He appeared satisfied, and I went on. I had
no chance either of exculpating myself, or
of probing the question to the bottom, but
by stating the naked truth, and therefore I
said at once, " Sarah told me, Sir (and I

never shall forget the way in which she told
me, fixing her dove's eyes upon me, and
looking a thousand tender reproaches for
the loss of that good opinion, which she
held dearer than all the world) she told me,
Sir, that as you one day passed the door,
which stood a-jar, you saw her in an attitude
which a good deal startled you; I mean
sitting in my lap, with her arms round my
neck, and mine twined round her in the
fondest manner. What I wished to ask was,
whether this was actually the case, or
whether it was a mere invention of her own,
to enhance the sense of my obligations to
her; for I begin to doubt everything?"—
"Indeed, it was so; and very much surprised and hurt I was to see it." "Well,
then, Sir, I can only say, that as you saw her
sitting then, so she had been sitting for the
last year and a half, almost every day of her
life, by the hour together; and you may
judge yourself, knowing what a nice modest-
looking girl she is, whether, after having
been admitted to such intimacy with so
sweet a creature, and for so long a time, it

is not enough to make anyone frantic to
be received by her as I have been since
my return, without any provocation given
or cause assigned for it." The old man
answered very seriously, and, as I think,
sincerely, "What you now tell me, Sir,
mortifies and shocks me, as much as it
can do yourself. I had no idea such a
thing was possible. I was much pained at
what I saw; but I thought it an accident,
and that it would never happen again."—
"It was a constant habit; it has happened
a hundred times since, and a thousand
before. I lived on her caresses as my daily
food, nor can I live without them." So I
told him the whole story, "what conjura-
tions, and what mighty magic I won his
daughter with," to be anything but *mine for
life*. Nothing could well exceed his astonishment and apparent mortification.
"What I had said," he owned, "had left
a weight upon his mind that he should not
easily get rid of." I told him, "For myself,
I never could recover the blow I had received. I thought, however, for her own

sake, she ought to alter her present behaviour. Her marked neglect and dislike,
so far from justifying, left her former inti-
macies without excuse; for nothing could
reconcile them to propriety, or even a pretence to common decency, but either love,
or friendship so strong and pure that it could
put on the guise of love. She was certainly
a singular girl. Did she think it right and
becoming to be free with strangers, and
strange to old friends?" I frankly declared,
"I did not see how it was in human nature
for any one who was not rendered callous to
such familiarities by bestowing them indiscriminately on every one, to grant the
extreme and continued indulgences she had
done to me, without either liking the man
at first, or coming to like him in the end, in
spite of herself. When my addresses had
nothing, and could have nothing honourable
in them, she gave them every encouragement; when I wished to make them honourable, she treated them with the utmost contempt. The terms we had been all along on
were such as if she had been to be my bride

next day. It was only when I wished her
actually to become so, to ensure her own
character and my happiness, that she shrunk
back with precipitation and panic-fear.
There seemed to me something wrong in all
this ; a want both of common propriety, and
I might say, of natural feeling ; yet, with all
her faults, I loved her, and ever should, beyond any other human being. I had drank
in the poison of her sweetness too long ever
to be cured of it ; and though I might find
it to be poison in the end, it was still in my
veins. My only ambition was to be permitted to live with her, and to die in her
arms. Be she what she would, treat me how
she would, I felt that my soul was wedded
to hers ; and were she a mere lost creature,
I would try to snatch her from perdition,
and marry her to-morrow if she would
have me. That was the question—" Would
she have me, or would she not ? " He
said he could not tell ; but should not
attempt to put any constraint upon her in-
clinations, one way or other. I acquiesced,
and added, that " I had brought all this

upon myself, by acting contrary to the
suggestions of my friend, Mr.——, who had
desired me to take no notice whether she
came near me or kept away, whether she
smiled or frowned, was kind or contemp-
tuous—all you have to do, is to wait patiently
for a month till you are your own man, as
you will be in all probability ; then make
her an offer of your hand, and if she re-
fuses, there's an end of the matter." Mr.
L. said, "Well, Sir, and I don't think you
can follow a better advice!" I took this
as a sort of negative encouragement, and so
we parted.

TO THE SAME *(in continuation).*

MY DEAR FRIEND,

The next day I felt almost as sailors must do after a violent storm overnight, that has subsided towards daybreak. The morning was a dull and stupid calm, and I found she was unwell, in consequence of what had happened. In the evening I grew more uneasy, and determined on going into the country for a week or two. I gathered up the fragments of the locket of her hair, and the little bronze statue, which were strewed about the floor, kissed them, folded them up in a sheet of paper, and sent them to her, with these lines written in pencil on the outside—"*Pieces of a broken heart, to be kept in remembrance of the unhappy. Farewell.*" No notice was taken ; nor did I expect any.

The following morning I requested Betsey to pack up my box for me, as I should go out of town the next day, and at the same time wrote a note to her sister to say, I should take it as a favour if she would please to accept of the enclosed copies of the *Vicar of Wakefield*, *The Man of Feeling*, and *Nature and Art*, in lieu of three volumes of my own writings, which I had given her on different occasions, in the course of our acquaintance. I was piqued, in fact, that she should have these to shew as proofs of my weakness, and as if I thought the way to win her was by plaguing her with my own performances. She sent me word back that the books I had sent were of no use to her, and that I should have those I wished for in the afternoon; but that she could not before, as she had lent them to her sister, Mrs. M——, I said, "Very well;" but observed (laughing) to Betsey, "It's a bad rule to give and take; so, if Sarah won't have these books, you must; they are very pretty ones, I assure you." She curtsied and took them, according to the family

custom. In the afternoon, when I came
back to tea, I found the little girl on her
knees, busy in packing up my things, and a
large paper-parcel on the table, which I
could not at first tell what to make of. On
opening it, however, I soon found what it
was. It contained a number of volumes
which I had given her at different times
(among others, a little Prayer-Book, bound
in crimson velvet, with green silk linings;
she kissed it twenty times when she received
it, and said it was the prettiest present in
the world, and that she would shew it to her
aunt, who would be proud of it)—and all
these she had returned together. Her name
in the title-page was cut out of them all. I
doubted at the instant whether she had done
this before or after I had sent for them back,
and I have doubted of it since; but there is
no occasion to suppose her *ugly all over with
hypocrisy*. Poor little thing! She has enough
to answer for, as it is. I asked Betsey if
she could carry a message for me, and she
said " *Yes*." " Will you tell your sister, then,
that I did not want all these books; and

give my love to her, and say that I shall be
obliged if she will still keep these that I
have sent back, and tell her that it is only
those of my own writing that I think unworthy of her." What do you think the
little imp made answer? She raised herself
on the other side of the table where she
stood, as if inspired by the genius of the
place, and said—"AND THOSE ARE THE ONES
THAT SHE PRIZES THE MOST!" If there
were ever words spoken that could revive
the dead, those were the words. Let me
kiss them, and forget that my ears have
heard aught else! I said, "Are you sure of
that?" and she said, "Yes, quite sure." I
told her, "If I could be, I should be very
different from what I was." And I became
so that instant, for these casual words carried
assurance to my heart of her esteem—that
once implied, I had proofs enough of her
fondness. Oh! how I felt at that moment!
Restored to love, hope, and joy, by a breath
which I had caught by the merest accident,
and which I might have pined in absence
and mute despair for want of hearing! I

did not know how to contain myself; I was childish, wanton, drunk with pleasure. I gave Betsey a twenty-shilling note which I happened to have in my hand, and on her asking "What's this for, Sir?" I said, "It's for you. Don't you think it worth that to be made happy? You once made me very wretched by some words I heard you drop, and now you have made me as happy; and all I wish you is, when you grow up, that you may find some one to love you as well as I do your sister, and that you may love better than she does me!" I continued in this state of delirium or dotage all that day and the next, talked incessantly, laughed at every thing, and was so extravagant, nobody could tell what was the matter with me. I murmured her name; I blest her; I folded her to my heart in delicious fondness; I called her by my own name; I worshipped her; I was mad for her. I told P—— I should laugh in her face, if ever she pretended not to like me again. Her mother came in and said, she hoped I should excuse Sarah's coming up. "Oh! Ma'am," I said,

"I have no wish to see her; I feel her at my heart; she does not hate me after all, and I wish for nothing. Let her come when she will, she is to me welcomer than light, than life; but let it be in her own sweet time, and at her own dear pleasure." Betsey also told me she was "so glad to get the books back." I, however, sobered and wavered (by degrees) from seeing nothing of her, day after day; and in less than a week I was devoted to the Infernal Gods. I could hold out no longer than the Monday evening following. I sent a message to her; she sent an ambiguous answer; but she came up. Pity me, my friend, for the shame of this recital. Pity me for the pain of having ever had to make it! If the spirits of mortal creatures, purified by faith and hope, can (according to the highest assurances) ever, during thousands of years of smooth-rolling eternity and balmy, sainted repose, forget the pain, the toil, the anguish, the helplessness, and the despair they have suffered here, in this frail being, then may I forget that withering hour, and her, that fair, pale form that entered, my inhuman betrayer, and my only earthly love! She said, "Did you wish to speak to me, Sir?" I said "Yes, may I not speak to you? I wanted to see you and be friends." I rose up, offered her an arm-chair which stood facing, bowed on it, and knelt to her adoring. She said (going) "If that's all, I have nothing to say." I replied, "Why do you treat me thus? What have I done to become thus hateful to you?" *Answer*, "I always told you I had no affection for you." You may suppose this was a blow, after the imaginary honeymoon in which I had passed the preceding week. I was stunned by it; my heart sunk within me. I contrived to say, "Nay, my dear girl, not always neither; for did you not once (if I might presume to look back to those happy, happy times) when you were sitting on my knee as usual, embracing and embraced, and I asked if you could not love me at last, did you not make answer, in the softest tones that ever man heard, '*I could easily say so, whether I did or not: you should judge by my actions!*' Was I to blame in

taking you at your word, when every hope I
had depended on your sincerity ? And did
you not say since I came back, '*Your feelings to me were the same as ever ?*' Why then
is your behaviour so different ?" S. "Is it
nothing, your exposing me to the whole
house in the way you did the other evening ?"
H. "Nay, that was the consequence of your
cruel reception of me, not the cause of it.
I had better have gone away last year, as I
proposed to do, unless you would give some
pledge of your fidelity ; but it was your own
offer that I should remain. 'Why should I
go ?' you said, 'Why could we not go on the
same as we had done, and say nothing about
the word *forever*?" S. "And how did you
behave when you returned ?" H. "That
was all forgiven when we last parted, and
your last words were, 'I should find you the
same as ever' when I came back ? Did you
not that very day enchant and madden me
over again by the purest kisses and embraces,
and did I not go from you (as I said) adoring, confiding, with every assurance of
mutual esteem and friendship ?" S. "Yes,

and in your absence I found that you had
told my aunt what had passed between us."
H. "It was to induce her to extort your
real sentiments from you, that you might no
longer make a secret of your true regard for
me, which your actions (but not your words)
confessed." S. "I own I have been guilty
of improprieties, which you have gone and
repeated, not only in the house, but out of
it; so that it has come to my ears from
various quarters, as if I was a light character. And I am determined in future to be
guided by the advice of my relations, and
particularly of my aunt, whom I consider as
my best friend, and keep every lodger at a
proper distance." You will find hereafter
that her favourite lodger, whom she visits
daily, had left the house; so that she might
easily make and keep this vow of extraordinary self-denial. Precious little dissembler!
Yet her aunt, her best friend, says, "No,
Sir, no; Sarah's no hypocrite!" which I was
fool enough to believe; and yet my great
and unpardonable offence is to have entertained passing doubts on this delicate point.

I said, Whatever errors I had committed, arose from my anxiety to have every thing explained to her honour; my conduct shewed that I had that at heart, and that I built on the purity of her character as on a rock. My esteem for her amounted to adoration. "She did not want adoration." It was only when any thing happened to imply that I had been mistaken, that I committed any extravagance, because I could not bear to think her short of perfection. "She was far from perfection," she replied, with an air and manner (oh, my God!) as near it as possible. "How could she accuse me of a want of regard to her? It was but the other day, Sarah," I said to her, "when that little circumstance of the books happened, and I fancied the expressions your sister dropped proved the sincerity of all your kindness to me—you don't know how my heart melted within me at the thought, that after all, I might be dear to you. New hopes sprung up in my heart, and I felt as Adam must have done when his Eve was created for him!" "She had heard enough of that sort of conversation," (moving towards the door). This, I own, was the unkindest cut of all. I had, in that case, no hopes whatever. I felt that I had expended words in vain, and that the conversation below stairs which I told you of when I saw you) had spoiled her taste for mine. If the allusion had been classical I should have been to blame ; but it was scriptural, it was a sort of religious courtship, and Miss L. is religious !

> At once he took his Muse and dipt her
> Right in the middle of the Scripture.

It would not do—the lady could make neither head nor tail of it. This is a poor attempt at levity. Alas ! I am sad enough. "Would she go and leave me so ? If it was only my own behaviour, I still did not doubt of success. I knew the sincerity of my love, and she would be convinced of it in time. If that was all, I did not care : but tell me true, is there not a new attachment that is the real cause of your estrangement ? Tell me, my sweet friend, and before you tell me, give me your hand (nay, both hands) that I

may have something to support me under
the dreadful conviction." She let me take
her hands in mine, saying, " She supposed
there could be no objection to that,"—as if
she acted on the suggestions of others,
instead of following her own will—but still
avoided giving me any answer. I conjured
her to tell me the worst, and kill me on the
spot. Any thing was better than my present
state. I said, " Is it Mr. C——?" She
smiled, and said with gay indifference, " Mr.
C—— was here a very short time." "Well,
then, was it Mr. ——?" She hesitated, and
then replied faintly, " No." This was a
mere trick to mislead ; one of the profound-
nesses of Satan, in which she is an adept.
" But," she added hastily, " she could make
no more confidences." " Then," said I,
" you have something to communicate."
" No ; but she had once mentioned a thing
of the sort, which I had hinted to her mother,
though it signified little." All this while I
was in tortures. Every word, every half-
denial, stabbed me. " Had she any tie ?"
" No, I have no tie ?" " You are not

going to be married soon?" "I don't intend ever to marry at all!" "Can't you be friends with me as of old?" "She could give no promises." "Would she make her own terms?" "She would make none."—"I was sadly afraid the *little image* was dethroned from her heart, as I had dashed it to the ground the other night." —"She was neither desperate nor violent." I did not answer—"But deliberate and deadly,"—though I might; and so she vanished in this running fight of question and answer, in spite of my vain efforts to detain her. The cockatrice, I said, mocks me: so she has always done. The thought was a dagger to me. My head reeled, my heart recoiled within me. I was stung with scorpions; my flesh crawled; I was choked with rage; her scorn scorched me like flames; her air (her heavenly air) withdrawn from me, stifled me, and left me gasping for breath and being. It was a fable. She started up in her own likeness, a serpent in place of a woman. She had fascinated, she had stung me, and had returned to her proper shape,

gliding from me after inflicting the mortal
wound, and instilling deadly poison into every
pore ; but her form lost none of its original
brightness by the change of character, but
was all glittering, beauteous, voluptuous
grace. Seed of the serpent or of the woman,
she was divine !   I felt that she was a witch,
and had bewitched me.   Fate had enclosed
me round about. *I* was transformed too,
no longer human (any more than she, to
whom I had knit myself) my feelings were
marble ; my blood was of molten lead ;
my thoughts on fire. I was taken out
of myself, wrapt into another sphere, far
from the light of day, of hope, of love. I
had no natural affection left ; she had slain
me, but no other thing had power over me.
Her arms embraced another ; but her mock-
embrace, the phantom of her love, still
bound me, and I had not a wish to escape.
So I felt then, and so perhaps shall feel till I
grow old and die, nor have any desire that
my years should last longer than they are
linked in the chain of those amorous folds,
or than her enchantments steep my soul in

oblivion of all other things! I started to
find myself alone—for ever alone, without a
creature to love me. I looked round the
room for help; I saw the tables, the chairs,
the places where she stood or sat, empty,
deserted, dead. I could not stay where I
was; I had no one to go to but to the
parent-mischief, the preternatural hag, that
had " drugged this posset " of her daughter's
charms and falsehood for me, and I went
down and (such was my weakness and
helplessness) sat with her for an hour, and
talked with her of her daughter, and the
sweet days we had passed together, and said
I thought her a good girl, and believed that
if there was no rival, she still had a regard
for me at the bottom of her heart; and how
I liked her all the better for her coy, maiden
airs : and I received the assurance over and
over that there was no one else ; and that
Sarah (they all knew) never staid five minutes
with any other lodger, while with me she
would stay by the hour together, in spite of
all her father could say to her (what were
her motives, was best known to herself!) and

while we were talking of her, she came
bounding into the room, smiling with smoth-
ered delight at the consummation of my
folly and her own art; and I asked her
mother whether she thought she looked as if
she hated me, and I took her wrinkled,
withered, cadaverous, clammy hand at parting,
and kissed it. Faugh!—

I will make an end of this story; there is
something in it discordant to honest ears. I
left the house the next day, and returned to
Scotland in a state so near to phrenzy, that
I take it the shades sometimes ran into one
another. R—— met me the day after I
arrived, and will tell you the way I was in.
I was like a person in a high fever; only
mine was in the mind instead of the body.
It had the same irritating uncomfortable
effect on the bye-standers. I was incapable
of any application, and don't know what I
should have done, had it not been for the
kindness of ——. I came to see you, to
" bestow some of my tediousness upon you,"
but you were gone from home. Every
thing went on well as to the law-business;

and as it approached to a conclusion, I wrote
to my good friend P—— to go to M——,
who had married her sister, and ask him if
it would be worth my while to make her a
formal offer, as soon as I was free, as, with
the least encouragement, I was ready to
throw myself at her feet; and to know, in
case of refusal, whether I might go back
there and be treated as an old friend. Not
a word of answer could be got from her on
either point, notwithstanding every impor-
tunity and intreaty; but it was the opinion
of M—— that I might go and try my fortune.
I did so with joy, with something like
confidence. I thought her giving no positive
answer implied a chance, at least, of the
reversion of her favour, in case I behaved
well. All was false, hollow, insidious. The
first night after I got home, I slept on down.
In Scotland, the flint had been my pillow.
But now I slept under the same roof with
her. What softness, what balmy repose in
the very thought! I saw her that same day
and shook hands with her, and told her how
glad I was to see her; and she was kind

and comfortable, though still cold and
distant. Her manner was altered from what
it was the last time. She still absented herself
from the room, but was mild and affable
when she did come. She was pale, dejected,
evidently uneasy about something, and had
been ill. I thought it was perhaps her
reluctance to yield to my wishes, her pity for
what I suffered ; and that in the struggle
between both, she did not know what to do.
How I worshipped her at these moments !
We had a long interview the third day, and
I thought all was doing well. I found her
sitting at work in the window-seat of the
front parlour ; and on my asking if I might
come in, she made no objection. I sat
down by her ; she let me take her hand ; I
talked to her of indifferent things, and of
old times. I asked her if she would put
some new frills on my shirts ?—" With
the greatest pleasure." If she could get
the little image mended ? " It was broken
in three pieces, and the sword was gone, but
she would try." I then asked her to make up
a plaid silk which I had given her in the

winter, and which she said would make a pretty summer gown. I so longed to see her in it!—"She had little time to spare, but perhaps might!" Think what I felt, talking peaceably, kindly, tenderly with my love,—not passionately, not violently. I tried to take pattern by her patient meekness, as I thought it, and to subdue my desires to her will. I then sued to her, but respectfully, to be admitted to her friendship—she must know I was as true a friend as ever woman had—or if there was a bar to our intimacy from a dearer attachment, to let me know it frankly, as I shewed her all my heart. She drew out her handkerchief and wiped her eyes " of tears which sacred pity had engendered there." Was it so or not? I cannot tell. But so she stood (while I pleaded my cause to her with all the earnestness and fondness in the world) with the tears trickling from her eye-lashes, her head stooping, her attitude fixed, with the finest expression that ever was seen of mixed regret, pity, and stubborn resolution; but without speaking a word, without altering

M

a feature. It was like a petrifaction of a
human face in the softest moment of passion.
"Ah!" I said, "how you look! I have
prayed again and again while I was away
from you, in the agony of my spirit, that I
might but live to see you look so again, and
then breathe my last!" I entreated her to
give me some explanation. In vain! At
length she said she must go, and disappeared
like a spirit. That week she did all the
little trifling favours I had asked of her.
The frills were put on, and she sent up to
know if I wanted any more done. She got
the Buonaparte mended. This was like
healing old wounds indeed! How? As
follows, for thereby hangs the conclusion of
my tale. Listen.

I had sent a message one evening to speak
to her about some special affairs of the house,
and received no answer. I waited an hour
expecting her, and then went out in great
vexation at my disappointment. I complained
to her mother a day or two after, saying I
thought it so unlike Sarah's usual propriety
of behaviour, that she must mean it as a mark

of disrespect. Mrs. L—— said, "La! Sir,
you're always fancying things. Why, she
was dressing to go out, and she was only
going to get the little image you're both
so fond of mended; and its to be done
this evening. She has been to two or
three places to see about it, before she could
get any one to undertake it." My heart, my
poor fond heart, almost melted within me at
this news. I answered, "Ah! Madam,
that's always the way with the dear creature.
I am finding fault with her and thinking the
hardest things of her; and at that very time
she's doing something to shew the most
delicate attention, and that she has no greater
satisfaction than in gratifying my wishes!"
On this we had some farther talk, and I took
nearly the whole of the lodgings at a hundred
guineas a year, that (as I said) she might
have a little leisure to sit at her needle of an
evening, or to read if she chose, or to walk
out when it was fine. She was not in good
health, and it would do her good to be less
confined. I would be the drudge and she
should no longer be the slave. I asked

nothing in return. To see her happy, to
make her so, was to be so myself.—This was
agreed to. I went over to Blackheath that
evening, delighted as I could be after all I had
suffered, and lay the whole of the next
morning on the heath under the open sky,
dreaming of my earthly Goddess. This was
Sunday. That evening I returned, for I
could hardly bear to be for a moment out of
the house where she was, and the next
morning she tapped at the door—it was
opened—it was she—she hesitated and then
came forward: she had got the little image
in her hand, I took it, and blest her from my
heart. She said "They had been obliged to
put some new pieces to it." I said "I didn't
care how it was done, so that I had it restored
to me safe, and by her." I thanked her and
begged to shake hands with her. She did so,
and as I held the only hand in the world that
I never wished to let go, I looked up in her
face, and said " Have pity on me, have pity
on me, and save me if you can!" Not a
word of answer, but she looked full in my
eyes, as much as to say, " Well, I'll think

of it; and if I can, I will save you!" We
talked about the expense of repairing the
figure. "Was the man waiting?"—" No,
she had fetched it on Saturday evening."
I said I'd give her the money in the course
of the day, and then shook hands with her
again in token of reconciliation; and she
went waving out of the room, but at the door
turned round and looked full at me, as she
did the first time she beguiled me of my
heart. This was the last.—

All that day I longed to go down stairs to
ask her and her mother to set out with me
for Scotland on Wednesday, and on Saturday
I would make her my wife. Something
withheld me. In the evening, however, I
could not rest without seeing her, and I said
to her younger sister, "Betsey, if Sarah will
come up now, I'll pay her what she laid out
for me the other day."—" My sister's gone
out, Sir," was the answer. What again!
thought I, That's somewhat sudden. I told
P—— her sitting in the window-seat of the
front parlour boded me no good. It was not
in her old character. She did not use to

know there were doors or windows in the
house—and now she goes out three times in
a week. It is to meet some one, I'll lay my
life on't. "Where is she gone?"—"To my
grandmother's, Sir." "Where does your
grandmother live now?"—"At Somers'
Town." I immediately set out to Somers'
Town. I passed one or two streets, and at
last turned up King-street, thinking it most
likely she would return that way home. I
passed a house in King-street where I had
once lived, and had not proceeded many
paces, ruminating on chance and change and
old times, when I saw her coming towards
me. I felt a strange pang at the sight, but
I thought her alone. Some people before
me moved on, and I saw another person with
her. *The murder was out.* It was a tall,
rather well-looking young man, but I did not
at first recollect him. We passed at the
crossing of the street without speaking.
Will you believe it, after all that had passed
between us for two years, after what had
passed in the last half-year, after what
had passed that very morning, she went

by me without even changing countenance,
without expressing the slightest emotion,
without betraying either shame or pity or
remorse or any other feeling that any
other human being but herself must have
shewn in the same situation. She had
no time to prepare for acting a part, to
suppress her feelings—the truth is, she has
not one natural feeling in her bosom to
suppress. I turned and looked—they also
turned and looked—and as if by mutual
consent, we both retrod our steps and passed
again, in the same way. I went home. I
was stifled. I could not stay in the house,
walked into the street, and met them coming
towards home. As soon as he had left her
at the door (I fancy she had prevailed with
him to accompany her, dreading some
violence) I returned, went upstairs, and
requested an interview. Tell her, I said, I'm
in excellent temper and good spirits, but I
must see her! She came smiling, and I said,
"Come in, my dear girl, and sit down, and
tell me all about it, how it is and who it
is."—"What," she said, "do you mean Mr.

C——?" "Oh," said I, "then it is he! Ah! you rogue, I always suspected there was something between you, but you know you denied it lustily: why did you not tell me all about it at the time, instead of letting me suffer as I have done? But however, no reproaches. I only wish it may all end happily and honourably for you, and I am satisfied. But," I said, "you know you used to tell me, you despised looks."—"She didn't think Mr. C—— was so particularly handsome." "No, but he's very well to pass, and a well-grown youth into the bargain." Pshaw! let me put an end to the fulsome detail. I found he had lived over the way, that he had been lured thence, no doubt, almost a year before, that they had first spoken in the street, and that he had never once hinted at marriage, and had gone away, because (as he said) they were too much together, and that it was better for her to meet him occasionally out of doors. "There could be no harm in their walking together." "No, but you may go some where afterwards."—"One must trust to

one's principle for that." Consummate
hypocrite! * * * * * * * * * * * * *
* * * * * * * * I told her Mr. M——,
who had married her sister, did not wish to
leave the house. I, who would have married
her, did not wish to leave it. I told her I
hoped I should not live to see her come to
shame, after all my love of her; but put her
on her guard as well as I could, and said,
after the lengths she had permitted herself
with me, I could not help being alarmed at
the influence of one over her, whom she
could hardly herself suppose to have a tenth
part of my esteem for her!! She made no
answer to this, but thanked me coldly for
my good advice, and rose to go. I begged
her to sit a few minutes, that I might try to
recollect if there was any thing else I
wished to say to her, perhaps for the last
time; and then, not finding any thing, I
bade her good night, and asked for a farewel kiss. Do you know she refused; so
little does she understand what is due to
friendship, or love, or honour! We parted
friends, however, and I felt deep grief, but

no enmity against her. I thought C——
had pressed his suit after I went, and had
prevailed. There was no harm in that—a
little fickleness or so, a little over-pretension
to unalterable attachment—but that was all.
She liked him better than me—it was my
hard hap, but I must bear it. I went out to
roam the desert streets, when, turning a
corner, whom should I meet but her very
lover ? I went up to him and asked for a
few minutes' conversation on a subject that
was highly interesting to me and I believed
not indifferent to him : and in the course
of four hours' talk, it came out that for
three months previous to my quitting
London for Scotland, she had been playing
the same game with him as with me—that
he breakfasted first, and enjoyed an hour of
her society, and then I took my turn, so
that we never jostled ; and this explained
why, when he came back sometimes and
passed my door, as she was sitting in my
lap, she coloured violently, thinking, if her
lover looked in, what a *denouement* there
would be. He could not help again and

again expressing his astonishment at finding that our intimacy had continued unimpaired up to so late a period after he came, and when they were on the most intimate footing. She used to deny positively to him that there was any thing between us, just as she used to assure me with impenetrable effrontery that " Mr. C——— was nothing to her, but merely a lodger." All this while she kept up the farce of her romantic attachment to her old lover, vowed that she never could alter in that respect, let me go to Scotland on the solemn and repeated assurance that there was no new flame, that there was no bar between us but .this shadowy love—I leave her on this understanding, she becomes more fond or more intimate with her new lover ; he quitting the house (whether tired out or not, I can't say)—in revenge she ceases to write to me, keeps me in wretched suspense, treats me like something loathsome to her when I return to enquire the cause, denies it with scorn and impudence, destroys me and shews no pity, no desire to soothe or shorten

the pangs she has occasioned by her
wantonness and hypocrisy, and wishes to
linger the affair on to the last moment,
going out to keep an appointment with
another while she pretends to be obliging
me in the tenderest point (which C——
himself said was too much)......What do
you think of all this ?   Shall I tell you my
opinion ?   But I must try to do it in another
letter.

TO THE SAME *(in Conclusion)*.

I did not sleep a wink all that night; nor did I know till the next day the full meaning of what had happened to me. With the morning's light, conviction glared in upon me that I had not only lost her for ever—but every feeling I had ever had towards her—respect, tenderness, pity—all but my fatal passion, was gone. The whole was a mockery, a frightful illusion. I had embraced the false Florimel instead of the true; or was like the man in the Arabian Nights who had married a *goul*. How different was the idea I once had of her! Was this she,

—" Who had been beguiled—she who was made
Within a gentle bosom to be laid—
To bless and to be blessed—to be heart-bare
To one who found his bettered likeness there—

To think for ever with him, like a bride—
To haunt his eye, like taste personified—
To double his delight, to share his sorrow,
And like a morning beam, wake to him every morrow?"

I saw her pale, cold form glide silent by me, dead to shame as to pity. Still I seemed to clasp this piece of witchcraft to my bosom : this lifeless image, which was all that was left of my love, was the only thing to which my sad heart clung. Were she dead, should I not wish to gaze once more upon her pallid features ? She is dead to me ; but what she once was to me, can never die ! The agony, the conflict of hope and fear, of adoration and jealousy is over ; or it would, ere long, have ended with my life. I am no more lifted now to Heaven, and then plunged in the abyss ; but I seem to have been thrown from the top of a precipice, and to lie groveling, stunned, and stupefied. I am melancholy, lonesome, and weaker than a child. The worst is, I have no prospect of any alteration for the better : she has cut off all possibility of a reconcilement at any

future period. Were she even to return to
her former pretended fondness and endearments, I could have no pleasure, no confidence in them. I can scarce make out the
contradiction to myself. I strive to think
she always was what I now know she is; but
I have great difficulty in it, and can hardly
believe but she still *is* what she so long
seemed. Poor thing! I am afraid she is
little better off herself; nor do I see what
is to become of her, unless she throws off
the mask at once, and *runs a-muck* at infamy.
She is exposed and laid bare to all those
whose opinion she set a value upon. Yet
she held her head very high, and must feel
(if she feels any thing) proportionably mortified. — A more complete experiment on
character was never made. If I had not
met her lover immediately after I parted
with her, it would have been nothing. I
might have supposed she had changed her
mind in my absence, and had given him the
preference as soon as she felt it, and even
shewn her delicacy in declining any farther
intimacy with me. But it comes out that

she had gone on in the most forward and
familiar way with both at once—(she could
not change her mind in passing from one
room to another)—told both the same bare-
faced and unblushing falsehoods, like the
commonest creature ; received presents from
me to the very last, and wished to keep up
the game still longer, either to gratify her
humour, her avarice, or her vanity in playing
with my passion, or to have me as a *dernier
resort*, in case of accidents.   Again, it would
have been nothing, if she had not come up
with her demure, well-composed, wheedling
looks that morning, and then met me in the
evening in a situation, which (she believed)
might kill me on the spot, with no more
feeling than a common courtesan shews,
who *bilks* a customer, and passes him, leer-
ing up at her bully, the moment after.   If
there had been the frailty of passion, it
would have been excusable ; but it is evident
she is a practised, callous jilt, a regular
lodging - house decoy, played off by her
mother upon the lodgers, one after another,
applying them to her different purposes,

laughing at them in turns, and herself the probable dupe and victim of some favourite gallant in the end. I know all this; but what do I gain by it, unless I could find some one with her shape and air, to supply the place of the lovely apparition? That a professed wanton should come and sit on a man's knee, and put her arms round his neck, and caress him, and seem fond of him, means nothing, proves nothing, no one concludes any thing from it; but that a pretty, reserved, modest, delicate-looking girl should do this, from the first hour to the last of your being in the house, without intending any thing by it, is new, and, I think, worth explaining. It was, I confess, out of my calculation, and may be out of that of others. Her unmoved indifference and self-possession all the while, shew that it is her constant practice. Her look even, if closely examined, bears this interpretation. It is that of studied hypocrisy or startled guilt, rather than of refined sensibility or conscious innocence. "She defied any one to read her thoughts?" she once told me.

N

"Do they then require concealing?" I imprudently asked her. The command over herself is surprising. She never once betrays herself by any momentary forgetfulness, by any appearance of triumph or superiority to the person who is her dupe, by any levity of manner in the plenitude of her success; it is one faultless, undeviating, consistent, consummate piece of acting. Were she a saint on earth, she could not seem more like one. Her hypocritical high-flown pretensions, indeed, make her the worse : but still the ascendancy of her will, her determined perseverance in what she undertakes to do, has something admirable in it, approaching to the heroic. She is certainly an extraordinary girl! Her retired manner, and invariable propriety of behaviour made me think it next to impossible she could grant the same favours indiscriminately to every one that she did to me. Yet this now appears to be the fact. She must have done the very same with C——, invited him into the house to carry on a closer intrigue with her, and then commenced the double

game with both together. She always " despised looks." This was a favourite phrase
with her, and one of the hooks which she
baited for me. Nothing could win her but
a man's behaviour and sentiments. Besides,
she could never like another—she was a
martyr to disappointed affection—and friendship was all she could even extend to any
other man. All the time, she was making
signals, playing off her pretty person, and
having occasional interviews in the street
with this very man, whom she could only
have taken so sudden and violent a liking to
from his looks, his personal appearance,
and what she probably conjectured of his
circumstances. Her sister had married a
counsellor—the Miss F——'s, who kept the
house before, had done so too—and so would
she. "There was precedent for it." Yet
if she was so desperately enamoured of this
new acquaintance, if he had displaced *the
little image* from her breast, if he was become
her *second* "unalterable attachment" (which
I would have given my life to have been)
why continue the same unwarrantable

familiarities with me to the last, and
promise that they should be renewed on my
return (if I had not unfortunately stumbled
upon the truth to her aunt)—and yet keep
up the same refined cant about her old
attachment all the time, as if it was that which
stood in the way of my pretensions, and not
her faithlessness to it? "If one swerves
from one, one shall swerve from another"—
was her excuse for not returning my regard.
Yet that which I thought a prophecy, was
I suspect a history. She had swerved twice
from her vowed engagements, first to me,
and then from me to another. If she made
a fool of me, what did she make of her lover?
I fancy he has put that question to himself.
I said nothing to him about the amount of
the presents; which is another damning
circumstance, that might have opened my
eyes long before; but they were shut by
my fond affection, which "turned all to
favour and to prettiness." She cannot be
supposed to have kept up an appearance
of old regard to me, from a fear of hurting
my feelings by her desertion; for she not

only shewed herself indifferent to, but
evidently triumphed in my sufferings, and
heaped every kind of insult and indignity
upon them. I must have incurred her
contempt and resentment by my mistaken
delicacy at different times; and her manner,
when I have hinted at becoming a reformed
man in this respect, convinces me of it.
"She hated it!" She always hated whatever
she liked most. She "hated Mr. C——'s
red slippers," when he first came! One
more count finishes the indictment. She
not only discovered the most hardened
indifference to the feelings of others; she
has not shewn the least regard to her own
character, or shame when she was detected.
When found out, she seemed to say, "Well,
what if I am? I have played the game as
long as I could; and if I could keep it up no
longer, it was not for want of good will!"
Her colouring once or twice is the only sign
of grace she has exhibited. Such is the
creature on whom I had thrown away my
heart and soul—one who was incapable of
feeling the commonest emotions of human

nature, as they regarded herself or any one else. "She had no feelings with respect to herself," she often said. She in fact knows what she is, and recoils from the good opinion or sympathy of others, which she feels to be founded on a deception; so that my overweening opinion of her must have appeared like irony, or direct insult. My seeing her in the street has gone a good way to satisfy me. Her manner there explains her manner in-doors to be conscious and overdone; and besides, she looks but indifferently. She is diminutive in stature, and her measured step and timid air do not suit these public airings. I am afraid she will soon grow common to my imagination, as well as worthless in herself. Her image seems fast "going into the wastes of time," like a weed that the wave bears farther and farther from me. Alas! thou poor hapless weed, when I entirely lose sight of thee, and forever, no flower will ever bloom on earth to glad my heart again!

THE END.

1893 INTRODUCTION.

THE RIGHT OF EDITORIAL DEDICATION
HAS RECENTLY BEEN CALLED IN QUESTION.
ALL THE SAME, IT HAS MUCH SUPPORT OF
NOTABLE EXAMPLE, ANCIENT AND MODERN;
AND, THEREFORE, AFTER THE FIRST OFFER-
ING OF THIS NEW EDITION OF THE "LIBER
AMORIS" TO THE HONOURED SHADE OF
HIM WHO MADE IT, I DESIRE TO ASSOCIATE
MY UNIMPORTANT SHARE IN ITS ISSUE
WITH THE NAME OF LORD DE TABLEY, IN
RESPECTFUL ADMIRATION OF HIS FINE
GIFTS AS A POET, AND EMBOLDENED BY A
FELLOWSHIP OF REGARD FOR THE GENIUS
OF WILLIAM HAZLITT.

R. LE G.

MAY 10, 1893.

INTRODUCTION.

If the reading of the "Liber Amoris" is not exactly a disappointment, at least it gives one a different kind of pleasure from that which we very probably expected. One looked, may be, for a beautiful garden of fancy, but soon found that the appeal was not so much to one's sense of beauty, as to one's curiosity, one's sense of humour, one's pity, sometimes even one's contempt. A few fine sentences are to be met with, but singularly few, and it is in fact not as literature, but as a document, "a document in madness," that the book has its value. Even had it not been written by Hazlitt it would have possessed this value, but in relation to him it becomes doubly interesting: for, at first sight, it seems that no aberration could have

been less characteristic of his morose and
unsympathetic nature. De Quincey tells us
that the book greatly raised Hazlitt in his
opinion, for this very reason " by shewing
him to be capable of stronger and more
agitating passions than " he " believed to be
within the range of his nature." All the
same, though erotic passion may have
seemed foreign to Hazlitt, he had passions
vehement enough in other directions. The
vehemence of his political passions was
notorious, his letter to Gifford was as fine
a burst of anger as can be imagined, and
he had a gift for misunderstanding his
friends, of taking petty slights, which was
continually hurrying him into ungovernable
rage.

He seems to have been incapable, in his
daily life, of taking broad views, and he
was as irritably alive to every little " insult,"
or semblance of it, as the most ignorant
young miss. When he imagined such, even
in the case of friends of proved loyalty,
he never stopped to think, never allowed
any sense of affection or gratitude to suggest

that he might be mistaken, but flew at once into absurd passion, and proceeded, if possible, to pillory the offender in his next essay. Mr. P. G. Patmore, in " My Friends and Acquaintance," gives several examples of this curious failing. You had only to accidentally pass him in the street, without having seen him, and he would at once decide that you had cut him, and go about seeking your scalp.

The persistent attacks upon him in *Blackwood's Magazine*, low and personal to a degree hardly realisable in our day, when we have seldom the excitement of a really spirited set-to among men of letters, and " knuckle-dusters" are forbidden, doubtless, aggravated this irritable self-consciousness. He could never forget that he was " pimpled Hazlitt," and the epithet made him skulk through the streets like a criminal, and made him especially sensitive in the presence of women, who, he felt sure, were always saying it over to themselves. It is impossible without a long quotation from Mr. Patmore, to give the reader any idea of the painful extremes of feeling to which this morbid sensitiveness subjected him.

For instance,—during the first week or fortnight after the appearance of (let us suppose) one of *Blackwood's* articles about him, if he entered a coffee-house where he was known, to get his dinner, it was impossible (he thought) that the waiters could be doing anything else all the time he was there, but pointing him out to guests as "the gentleman who was so abused last month in *Blackwood's Magazine*." If he knocked at the door of a friend, the look and reply of the servant (whatever they might be), made it evident to him that he had been reading *Blackwood's Magazine* before the family were up in the morning ! If he had occasion to call at any of the publishers for whom he might be writing at the time, the case was still worse,—inasmuch as there his bread was at stake, as well as that personal civility, which he valued no less. Mr. Colburn would be "not within," as a matter of course ; for his clerks to even ascertain his pleasure on that point beforehand would be wholly superfluous : had they not all chuckled over the article at their tea the evening before ? Even the instinct of the shop-boys would catch the cue from the significant looks of those above them, and refuse to take his name to Mr. Ollier. They would "believe he was gone to dinner." He could not, they thought, want to have anything to say to a person who, as it were, went about with a sheet of *Black-*

wood's pinned to his coat-tail like a dish-clout!

Then at home at his lodgings, if the servant who waited upon him did not answer his bell the first time — Ah! 'twas clear—She had read *Blackwood's*, or heard talk of it at the bar of the public-house when she went for the beer! Did the landlady send up his bill a day earlier than usual, or ask for payment of it less civilly than was her custom—how could he wonder at it? It was *Blackwood's* doing. But if she gave him notice to quit (on the score, perhaps, of his inordinately late hours) he was a lost man! for would anybody take him in after having read *Blackwood's*? Even the strangers that he met in the streets seemed to look at him askance, "with jealous leer malignant," as if they knew him by intuition for a man on whom was set the double seal of public and private infamy; the doomed and denounced of *Blackwood's Magazine*.

An inherent lack of humour was probably the spring of Hazlitt's defects. Mr. Patmore says too that "an ingrained selfishness, more or less influenced or modified all the other points of his nature," and certainly the general complexion of Hazlitt's life seems at least to have been that of gloomy self-absorption. However, it will be fair here to recall Barry Cornwall's more

complete and certainly more generous view
of his character :—

Hazlitt himself had strong passions, and a few
prejudices ; and his free manifestations of these were
adduced as an excuse for the slander and animosity
with which he was perpetually assailed.   He attacked
others, indeed (a few only), and of these he expressed
his dislike in terms sometimes too violent perhaps,
and at no time to be mistaken.   Yet, when an
opportunity arose to require from him an unbiassed
opinion, he was always just.   He did not carry
poisoned arrows into civil conflict.   Subject to the
faults arising out of this, his warm temperament, he
possessed qualities worthy of affection and respect.
He was a simple, unselfish man, void of all deception
and pretence; and he had a clear, acute intellect,
when not traversed by some temporary passion or
confused by a strong prejudice.... Like many others,
he was sometimes swayed by his affections.   He loved
the first Napoleon beyond the bounds of reason.   He
loved the worker better than the idler.   He hated
pretensions supported merely by rank or wealth or
repute, or by the clamour of factions.   And he felt
love and hatred in an intense degree.   But he was
never dishonest.   He never struck down the weak,
nor trod on the prostrate.   He was never treacherous,
never tyrannical, never cruel......

My first meeting with Mr. Hazlitt took place at the

house of Leigh Hunt, where I met him at supper. I expected to see a severe, defiant-looking being. I met a grave man, diffident, almost awkward in manner, whose appearance did not impress me with much respect. He had a quick, restless eye, however, which opened eagerly when any good or bright observation was made; and I found at the conclusion of the evening, that when any question arose, the most sensible reply always came from him. Although the process was not too obvious, he always seemed to have reasoned with himself before he uttered a sentence.

There is no doubt that his strong passions and determined likings often interfered with his better reason. His admiration of Napoleon would not allow of any qualification.

And then Barry Cornwall refers to the frenzy which was the *raison d'être* of the following pages, a reference which will be of interest to us later on.

The following sonnet by Sheridan Knowles printed, *à propos* of Bewick's chalk drawing of Hazlitt, reproduced in front of his son's edition of his " Literary Remains," is of value as the testimony of a man who knew him intimately, and was, indeed, with Patmore, the sharer of his confidences in

regard to that divine impossible she, Sarah
Walker :—

Thus Hazlitt looked ! There's life in every line !
  Soul—language—fire that colour could not give,
See ! on that brow how pale-robed thought divine,
  In an embodied radiance seems to live !
Ah ! in the gaze of that entrancèd eye,
  Humid, yet burning, there beams passion's flame,
  Lighting the cheek, and quivering through the
      frame ;
While round the lips, the odour of a sigh
  Yet hovers fondly, and its shadow sits
Beneath the channel of the glowing thought
  And fire-clothed eloquence, which comes in fits
Like Pythiac inspiration !—Bewick taught
  By thee, in vain doth slander's venom'd dart
  Do its foul work 'gainst *him*. This head *must* own
      a heart.

Hazlitt's face in this portrait wears certainly
a sensibility of expression, almost amounting
to voluptuousness, such as appears but little
if at all in his portrait by his brother. Bewick thus helps us the better to understand
the " Liber Amoris."

We have seen that Hazlitt was in other
directions a man of strong passions, and

the man who is passionate in one thing may be passionate in any when the spark falls. But, actually, Hazlitt had always been susceptible to woman. Patmore, giving an account of his curious daily habits, tells us how, rising at one or two, he would sit over his breakfast of black tea and toast (his slavery to black tea had, doubtless, much to do with his misanthropy) "silent, motionless, and self - absorbed," till the evening, oppressed by a *vis inertiæ*, which he was incapable of resisting, unless at the prospect of absolute destitution (for he never wrote till necessity actually forced it upon him) or "moved to do so by some inducement in which *female* attraction had a chief share." Patmore also makes a mysterious reference to a walk home one evening with Hazlitt, during which, in the "broad part of Parliament Street, opposite to the Admiralty and the Horse Guards," Hazlitt was addressed by "sundry petitioners," *filles de joie* in fact, apparently acquainted with him, and whose acquaintance he did not affect to disown.

Again, in writing of the evenings spent at the Southampton Coffee-house, Patmore, dwelling on Barry Cornwall's share in them, says :—

And, above all other themes, to P[rocte]r, and to him alone (except myself) Hazlitt could venture to relate, in all their endless details those " affairs of the heart " in one of which his *head* was always engaged, and which happily always (with one fatal exception) evaporated in that interminable talk about them of which he was so strangely fond.

Not that Hazlitt confined his confidences on this head to P[rocte]r and myself. On the contrary, he extended them to almost every individual with whom he had occasion to speak, if he could, by hook or crook, find or make the occasion of bringing in the topic. But, in general, he did this from a sort of physical incapacity to avoid the favourite yet dreaded theme of his thoughts ; and he did it with a perfect knowledge that his confidential communications were a *bore* to nine-tenths of those who listened to them, and consequently that the pleasure of the communication was anything but mutual.... The truth is that Hazlitt *was* a child in this matter ; yet at the same time he was a metaphysician, a philosopher, and a poet ; and hence the (in my mind) curious and unique interest which attached to his mingled details and dissertations on this the most favourite of all his themes of converse, at least in a *tête à tête* ; for he rarely, if ever, brought up the subject under any other circumstances.

But long before the days of "The South-ampton," Hazlitt appears to have had an experience no less violent in its excess than that "one fatal exception," which is, of course, that celebrated in the present volume. He was then, however, more of an age for such experience, being, apparently, about twenty. The affair happened up at the lakes, during a visit to Wordsworth, whose friendship, as also Southey's, and perhaps Coleridge's too, it cost him. Patmore gives the most significant account of it, and I cannot do better than quote him once more :—

I allude, he says, to a story relating to Hazlitt's alleged treatment of some petty village jilt, who, when he was on a visit to Wordsworth, had led him (Hazlitt) to believe that she was not insensible to his attractions ; and then, having induced him to "com-mit" himself to her in some ridiculous manner, turned round upon him, and made him the laughing-stock of the village. There is, I believe, too much truth in the statement of his enemies, that the

mingled disappointment and rage of Hazlitt on this
occasion led him, during the madness of the moment
(for it must have been nothing less), to acts which
nothing but the supposition of insanity could account
for, much less excuse. And his conduct on this
occasion is understood to have been the immediate
cause of that breach between him and his friends
above-named (at least Wordsworth and Southey),
which was never afterwards healed.

Here we catch a glimpse of that dæmonic
frenzy which later on seems, and no wonder,
to have agitated even the phlegmatic nerves
of Sarah Walker. Lamb makes a waggish
allusion to the incident in a letter to Wordsworth during 1814, from which we gather
that Hazlitt narrowly missed a ducking
in the horse-pond for his eccentricities.
Wordsworth had evidently been writing
Lamb on the subject.

The "scapes" of the great god Pan, who appeared
among your mountains some dozen years since, and
his narrow chance of being submerged by the swains,
afforded me much pleasure. I can conceive the
water-nymphs pulling for him. He would have
been another Hylas — W. Hylas. In a mad letter
which Capel Lofft wrote to M[onthly] M[agazine],
Philips (now Sir Richard), I remember his noticing

a metaphysical article of Pan, signed H., and adding "I take your correspondent to be the same with Hylas." Hylas had put forth a pastoral just before. How near the unfounded conjecture of the certainly inspired Lofft (unfounded as we thought) was to being realised ! I can conceive him being "good to all that wonder in that perilous flood !"

De Quincey used to hint also that Hazlitt was attached to Miss Wordsworth, the poet's sister, Dorothy, but Mr. W. C. Hazlitt thinks that very little stress must be laid on the conjecture.

The next authentic name in the legend of Hazlitt's loves is that of Miss Railton, of Liverpool. Her father was a friend of Hazlitt's father, and when William went touring as a roving portrait painter through the provinces, he gave him one or two commissions. It was not William, however, but his brother John, the miniature-painter, who has preserved for us the "very dark dangerous eyes" of Miss Railton. She was about twenty-five when Hazlitt first met her— about his own age—and he seems to have been very much in love. But a match with a struggling artist did not commend itself to the parents of the lady, and so the affair came to nothing.

Another name, presented to us merely by a bantering allusion of his wife, was "Sally Shepherd." Mr. W. C. Hazlitt says that Mrs. Hazlitt would "tax him from time to time with having had a sweetness once for Sally Shepherd," and that the only conjecture as to the owner of this pretty name is that she was perhaps the daughter of Dr. Shepherd of Gateacre, whose portrait he painted in 1803.

Still another lady seems to have swayed the ardent soul of William Hazlitt: Miss Windham, only daughter of the Hon. Charles Windham, of Norman Court, near Salisbury. She is described as having been very handsome, though pitted with smallpox, and we are told that a lady once remarking to Hazlitt—what a terrible disfigurement smallpox was, he had replied that the most beautiful woman he ever knew was so marked, and, lowering his voice, he mentioned the name of Miss Windham. Miss Windham, however, married otherwhere, and, curiously

enough, when Hazlitt came to live at Winterslow, in their near neighbourhood, her
husband offered him the free use of apart-
ments in Norman Court — an offer such
as Hazlitt's (somewhat small) pride could,
under no circumstances, have entertained.
In one of his essays he has a pathetic
apostrophe beginning: "Ye woods, that
crown the clear low brow of Norman Court,"
in which he speaks of "that face, pale as
the primrose, with hyacinthine locks, for
ever shunning and for ever haunting me.."

However, Hazlitt's fate, as the gipsies
say, seemed to lie about Winterslow. A
certain Dr. Stoddart and his sister Sarah
lived in retirement on a small property there.
Dr. Stoddart was a friend of John Hazlitt's,
and he and Miss Stoddart were also friends
of the Lambs. William would thus naturally
become acquainted with Sarah, though we
have no record of his first introduction to
her. Mary Lamb and Sarah Stoddart seem
indeed to have been quite intimate friends,
and it is only through Mary's letters to Sarah
that we catch any glimpses of the develop-

ment of relations between Sarah and William. Indeed, one cannot quite absolve Mary from indulgence in that alluring game of match-making. Could it have been of the gentle Mary that Hazlitt was thinking when in his "Advice to a Schoolboy," he bids his son beware, in the choice of a wife, of meddle-some friends ?

We gather from a letter of hers, dated 21st September, 1803, that Sarah was then engaged to another, but that she was of two minds whether or not to jilt him for William. Mary begins by advising her " to drop all correspondence with William," but ends in this strain : " God bless you, and grant you may preserve your integrity, and remain unmarried and penniless, and make William a good and happy wife." Early in 1804, we find the good Mary slyly hinting at the subject again : " Rickman wants to know if you are going to be married yet. Satisfy him in that little par-ticular when you write."

I should say that towards the end of 1803 Dr. Stoddart had, as a professional specu-

lation, settled, with his sister, in Malta, at
the time Coleridge made his ill-fated expedition there.   In thanking Sarah for news
of Coleridge's safe arrival, Mary cannot
resist further allusions to what would really
seem to have been a pet project with her.
Dr. Stoddart's venture apparently had not
been successful.   " I cannot condole with
you very sincerely," writes Mary, "upon
your little failure in the fortune - making
way. If you regret it, so do I.   But I hope
to see you a comfortable English wife, and
the forsaken, forgotten William, of English
partridge memory, I have still a hankering
after..... I trust you will at last find some
man who has sense enough to know you are
well worth risking a probable life of poverty
for. I shall yet live to see you a poor, but
happy English wife."   The allusion to
partridges is an extinct joke to-day, but it
had evidently tickled Mary, for in September
1805 it was still alive.   " Has the partridge
season opened any communication between
you and William ?" wrote Mary. "As I allow
you to be imprudent till I see you, I shall

expect to hear you have invited him to taste his own birds. Have you scratched him out of your will yet?"

A month or two later we read: "I want to know if you have seen William, and if there is any prospect in future there. All you said in your letter from Portsmouth that related to him was burnt so in the fumigating" [for disinfecting purposes] "that we could only make out that it was unfavourable, but not the particulars. Tell us again how you go on, and if you have seen him. I conceit affairs will somehow he made up between you at last."

Space forbids that we follow Miss Stoddart through all the ups and downs of her variable affections. Her vacillations continued for another three years, a Mr. White and a Mr. Dowling being added to the game, or ever the tale was told. However, in the long run Mary Lamb was to have her wish, though, like many who have contributed to an event, she seems to have grown a little anxious as it really approached. Toward the end of 1807 she writes: "Farewell! Determine

as wisely as you can in regard to Hazlitt;
and if your determination is to have him,
heaven send you many happy years together,
....if I were sure you would not be quite
starved to death, nor beaten to a mummy,
I should like to see Hazlitt and you come
together, if (as Charles observes) it were
only for the joke sake."

The joke came off on the 1st of May,
1808, at St. Andrew's Church, Holborn.
The Lambs were at the marriage, and,
writing to Southey seven years after, Lamb
thus alludes to it: "I was at Hazlitt's
marriage, and had like to have been turned
out several times during the ceremony.
Anything awful makes me laugh."

The first and only fruits of their union
was the birth on the 26 September, 1811, of
their son William, who was soon to be the
only bond between them.

It was necessary thus to sketch the story
of Hazlitt's heart prior to his meeting the
heroine of *Liber Amoris* because of the light
it throws upon his temperament, and also
upon his relations with his wife.

We have seen that Miss Stoddart did not
accept him before she had flirted consider-
ably with others, and one is bound to feel
in reading Mr. W. C. Hazlitt's "Memoirs,"
that these flirtations were not the attractions
of an ardent temperament, but merely the
experiments of a worldly one. She seems
to have been a woman of amiable enough
disposition and even exceptionally cultured
—though she does not seem to have
sympathised with her husband's work—but
utterly matter-of-fact and devoid of poetic
sensibility. She hadn't a half-pennyworth
of romantic love in her. An extra thousand
a year, apparently, would have moved her
heart beyond the most heroic devotion; and
we can but conclude that she accepted
Hazlitt as a forlorn hope. Yet she was a
good wife, so far as wifely duty goes, and
especially a good mother. The rift between
them was in the absolute lack of tempera-
mental sympathy. So far as one can make
out she was a better wife than Hazlitt was a
husband; for Hazlitt must have been very
difficult to live with, and though of actual

inconstancy we have no hint, it was against his nature to remain long constant to one affection.

In his edition of his father's literary remains, young William Hazlitt speaks of the failure of mutual happiness between his father and mother, "owing in great measure to an imagined and most unfounded idea, on my father's part, of a want of sympathy on that of my mother."

Whosoever the fault mostly was, the fact remains that Hazlitt and his wife were an uncomfortable pair, and before the autumn of 1819 we find them living apart.

And here we at last arrive at the print-dress divinity celebrated in the following pages.

In letter IV. one reads of "the time I first saw the sweet apparition, August 16, 1820." The "sweet apparition" was Sarah Walker, daughter of a Mr. Walker, tailor and lodging-house keeper at No. 9, Southampton Buildings, Chancery Lane, where Hazlitt had come to take up his solitary abode. The superstitious reader may notice that the

name Sarah seems to have been of sinister
significance to Hazlitt's fate : Sarah Shepherd, Sarah Stoddart, and now Sarah Walker.
Mr. W. C. Hazlitt says that Mr. Walker had
two daughters, but surely he had three, for
in "The Quarrel" (p. 18), arising out of
Sarah's little sister Betsey playing eaves-
dropper to the embraces of the fond lovers,
Sarah speaks of an eldest sister, and implies
her marriage to "Mr. M———." De Quincey,
too, says that "her sister had married very
much above her rank." Obviously he could
not have been referring to little Betsey, but
to the wife of "Mr. M———." Mr. W. C.
Hazlitt says that Betsey Walker afterwards
married a gentleman named Roscoe, whom,
however, he identifies with "Mr. M.———."
In 1822 Hazlitt writes to his friend (Letter
XII. p. 99) asking him "to call on M———
in confidence." In the original MS. of this
in "Memoirs" the blank reads "to call on
Roscoe in confidence," and Mr. W. C. Hazlitt remarks in a foot-note : "the gentleman
who had married the sister, and was said to
be very happy in his choice"—the "sister"

being apparently Betsey, who, according to the *Liber Amoris*, was still a little girl! Evidently there is some confusion here, which can only be explained by Sarah having two sisters, or on the supposition that Hazlitt invented the Flibbertigget little sister for dramatic purposes. But that seems very improbable, and quite out of keeping with the general treatment of his confession, which is all through marked with a quite sordid adherence to fact. Besides, the petty humiliation of the child's running out of hiding, and saying "He thought I did not see him!" is too lifelike for invention. It makes one blush with pity for the poor nympholepht, reduced by his passion to such degrading familiarities.

For descriptions of Sarah Walker, probably the most absurdly idealised of all literary goddesses—which is saying much—we are not entirely dependent on Hazlitt's raptures. Barry Cornwall describes her with some care, and I cannot do better than quote the whole passage, as it gives the completest and most circumstantial account of Hazlitt's frenzy left by his contemporaries :—

His intellect was completely subdued by an insane passion. He was, for a time, unable to think or talk of anything else. He abandoned criticism and books as idle matters, and fatigued every person whom he met by expressions of her love, of her deceit, and of his own vehement disappointment. This was when he lived in Southampton Buildings, Holborn. Upon one occasion I know that he told the story of his attachment to five different persons in the same day. And at each time entered into minute details of his love-story. "I am a cursed fool," said he to me. "I saw I—— going into Wills' Coffee-house yesterday morning; he spoke to me. I followed him into the house, and whilst he lunched I told him the whole story. Then I wandered into the Regent's Park, where I met one of M——'s sons. I walked with him some time, and on his using some civil expressions, by Jove, Sir, I told him the whole story!" [Here he mentioned another instance which I forget.] "Well, sir" (he went on), "I then went and called on Hayden, but he was out. There was only his man, Salmon, there; but by Jove! I could not help myself. It all came out; the whole cursed story. Afterwards I went to look at some lodgings at Pimlico. The landlady at one place, after some explanations as to rent, &c., said to me very kindly, "I am afraid you are not well Sir?" "No, Ma'am," said I, "I am not well;" and on enquiring further, the devil take

me if I did not let out the whole story from beginning
to end." I used to see this girl, Sarah Walker, at
his lodgings, and could not account for the extravagant
passion of her admirer. She was the daughter of the
lodging-house-keeper. Her face was round and small,
and her eyes were motionless, glassy, and without
any speculation (apparently) in them. Her movements in walking were very remarkable, for I never
observed her to make a step. She went onwards in
a sort of wavy, sinuous manner, like the movements
of a snake. She was silent, or uttered monosyllables
only, and was very demure. Her steady, unmoving
gaze upon the person whom she was addressing was exceedingly unpleasant. The Germans would have extracted a romance from her, enduing her perhaps with
some diabolic attribute. To this girl he gave all his
valuable time, all his wealth of thought, and all the
loving frenzy of his heart. For a time I think that
on this point he was substantially insane—certainly
beyond self-control. To him she was a being full of
witching, full of grace, with all the capacity of
tenderness. The retiring coquetry, which had also
brought others to her, invested her in his sight with
the attractions of a divinity.

Making allowance for the fact that in
almost every passion,

> "some hidden hand
> Reveals to him that loveliness
> Which others cannot understand,"

it seems to me from this description,
written, one must not forget, in cold blood,
that Sarah Walker was physically by no
means unattractive. She was evidently a
sensuous creature, not unskilled in the arts
of the body. That sinuous movement, that
gliding walk, that general suggestion of
Melusine, may well have appealed to a man
so predisposed to erotomania as Hazlitt, and
before we dismiss Hazlitt's conception of
her charms as entirely hallucination De Quincey does well to remind us that Hazlitt's
" eye had been long familiar with the beauty
(real and ideal) of the painters." De Quincey also adds another touch to her portrait.
Hazlitt had confessed, he said, in conversation that one characteristic of her complexion
made somewhat against her charm, " that
she had a look of being somewhat jaded,
as if she were unwell, or the freshness of
the animal sensibilities gone by." May not
this have been the passion-pallor, so much
in evidence in aesthetic poetry—another
mark of a strongly sexual nature.

Whatever may have been the truth about

her physical charms, Hazlitt certainly attributed to her spiritual, moral and mental qualities which she was far from possessing. For us, who have no opportunity of appreciating the glamour of her walk, and can only judge her by her talk, she seems the very type of a servant girl. Predisposed to immorality, yet she is full of petty conventionality, of sententious propriety, very nice of her "honour," studiously sensitive of "insult," "has no secrets from her mother," and cannot be more to him than a friend, allows no "liberties," and yet has no scruples about sitting by the hour on lodgers' knees. She is lumpish, unresponsive, full of ignorant pride, and is, of course, no little pious.

Towards the end Hazlitt began to see her more in this light. He calls her "little yes and no," and even so early as Letter II., in a fit of pique, he is impious enough to exclaim : "After all, what is there in her but a pretty figure, and that you can't get a word out of her?" A momentary gleam of sane criticism. On one occasion even a gleam of humour breaks from his owlish absorption.

"I have high ideas of the married state !" says the sententious little hussey.

"Higher than of the maiden state ?" asks Hazlitt slyly, irony which nearly lost him his parting kiss.

If she was a tradesman's daughter, she had as nice a sense of honour, &c. "Talk of a tradesman's daughter," cries the en- amoured essayist, with a confusion of pro- nouns often observable in emotion of the kind—"you would ennoble any family, thou glorious girl by true nobility of mind."

Hazlitt had met Sarah Walker, August 16, 1820. Later in the same year, or early in 1821, the idea of a formal separation between him and his wife seems first to have been mentioned, but no steps seem to have been taken till early in 1822, when we find Hazlitt in Scotland. The original MS of the "Liber Amoris," in the possession of Mr. W. C. Hazlitt, is dated Stamford, January 29, 1822. "I was detained at Stamford," he says in his first letter, "and found myself dull, and could hit upon no other way of employing my time so agreeably." Hazlitt remained in

Scotland, with the exception of a freakish journey Londonwards (see Letter to J. S. K.) till about July 18. Meanwhile he had lived partly at Edinburgh, partly at Renton Inn (the " Bees Inn " of the " Liber Amoris ") in Berwickshire. At Renton Inn he wrote a whole volume of his " Table Talk " (see Letter X.). Mrs. Hazlitt landed at Leith on April 21, and with her coming the arrangements for divorce seem to have been accelerated. On May 6, Hazlitt lectured at Glasgow on Milton and Shakespeare, and on May 13 on Thomson and Burns. On June 17 Mrs. Hazlitt went for a short tour in the Highlands, returning to Edinburgh on June 28. The divorce seems to have been settled on July 17, as Hazlitt sailed for London on the 18th, and Mrs. Hazlitt on the 19th of that month.

It is unnecessary for me to dwell on the details of the divorce, or of the time spent in Edinburgh pending it, as (owing to the kindness of Mr. W. C. Hazlitt), I have been able to reprint the whole of the extracts from Mrs. Hazlitt's diary of the time, first printed in "The Memoirs." This will enable the reader to fill in for himself the background to certain allusions to Hazlitt's Edinburgh exile in the "Liber Amoris."

It is surely one of the most curious documents in the history of "love." The whole affair is seen to have been so purely a matter of business with them. It certainly throws a light on the incompatibility of their union. Mrs. Hazlitt had, doubtless, many good qualities, but this diary reveals a coldness of temperament which, when we remember Hazlitt's subterranean volcanoes, goes far to explain their want of sympathy. A little temper would have been a hopeful sign. But, no! they are each evidently too pleased at the prospect of release for that. So they talk pictures and take tea together like old friends, and, one must add, like sensible people. The only touch of feeling is in reference to their child. Whatever love they ever had for each other centres in it.

One quaint incident of the affair, not mentioned either in Mrs. Hazlitt's diary or

" The Memoirs," is to be found in Forster's
"Life of Landor." The anecdote was related
in a letter from Seymour Kirkup to John
Forster. Hazlitt, on his second wedding
tour, paid a visit to Landor at the Palazzo
Medici, in the spring of 1825.

" As Hazlitt's present continental journey," wrote
Kirkup, " was in the nature of a holiday wedding-trip
with his second wife, whose small independence had
enabled him to give himself that unusual enjoyment,
he appears to have had no scruple in dilating to his
friends on those facilities of Scottish law which had
opened to him such advantages."

" He related to Landor, Brown and myself one day
the history of his own divorce. He told us that he
and his wife, having always some quarrel going on,
determined at last, from incompatibility of temper, to
get separated. So, to save Mrs. H.'s honour, and
have all their proceedings legal, they went to work in
this way. They took the steamboat to Leith, pro-
vided themselves each with good law advice, and
continued on the most friendly terms in Edinburgh
till everything was ready ; when Hazlitt described
himself calling in from the streets a not very respectable female confederate, and for form's sake, putting
her in his bed and lying down beside her. ' Well,
sir,' said Hazlitt, turning more particularly to Landor,
who had by this time thrown out signs of the most

lively interest, ' down I lay, and the folding-doors
opened, and in walked Mrs. H., accompanied by two
gentlemen.   She turned to them and said : Gentlemen, do you know who that person is in that bed
along with that woman ?   Yes, madam, they politely
replied, 'tis Mr. William Hazlitt.   On which, sir, she
made a courtesy, and they went out of the room, and
left me and my companion *in statu quo*.   She and
her witnesses then accused me of adultery, sir, and
obtained a divorce against me, which, by gad, sir,
was a benefit to both."

We are told that Landor listened to this
story with " eager anxiety," and hailed its
conclusion with " irrepressible delight."
" On other points, too," adds Kirkup,
" Hazlitt and his host found themselves in
unaccustomed yet perfect sympathy ; and so
heartily did each enjoy the other's wilfulness
and caprice, that a strong personal liking
characterised their brief acquaintance."

Does this odd story mean that these
business-like people had or had not a sense
of humour ?   While these legalities were
trailing their slow length along, Hazlitt's soul
was pouring out his fiery love for Sarah Walker
in the letters which chiefly compose the

following pages. The majority of them were
written to Mr. P. G. Patmore, who is the
"C.P." of the series.   Mr. Patmore published
a selection from the original versions in "My
Friends and Acquaintances," and that I am
fortunately able to reprint here, so that the
reader may compare the two versions for
himself.   He will remark that two or three
of the letters in the "Liber Amoris" are
out of their proper order.

The two final letters to " J.S.K—" were
written to James Sheridan Knowles, the
dramatist, who regarded Hazlitt with something like hero-worship.   In a letter to Mr.
Patmore not included either in "My Friends
and Acquaintances," or the "Liber Amoris"
(see Appendix, p. lxxxix.) and probably
written between June 3rd and 9th, Hazlitt
says "I am going to see K——, to get him
to go with me to the Highlands, and talk
about *her*."   A cheerful prospect for poor
Knowles! However, "K——" seems to
have proved himself a friend in a thousand,
and to have suffered his friend's maunderings
with an unexampled fortitude.   The reader

will find references to their Highland walks
and talks on pages 121—125, pages too
in which one gains grateful glimpses of
the more robust Hazlitt, who wrote so finely
on walking tours. With the bracing in-
fluences of Highland scenery around him,
Sarah Walker was not quite without a rival,
and Hazlitt seems to have been not so
trying a companion after all.

This letter to " J.S.K." gives so literal a
version of the conclusion of Hazlitt's
passion that there is no necessity for me to
recapitulate it here. Suffice it that on his
return to London, he humiliated himself
before her to a still more ludicrous degree,
and on her still remaining a Galatea no
prayers could warm to life, gave way to
frenzies of passion that very naturally
alarmed the whole Walker household. This
seems to have been the final flare-up of his
feelings, for on his suddenly discovering
that his old fellow lodger, had, as he suspected, been her lover all the time, he gives
up the game as suddenly as he took it up,
and we leave him talking the calmest philo-

sophy, with an eye that is already beginning to suspect a humorous side to the whole absurd drama. " Her image," he says, "seems fast 'going into the wastes of time' like a weed that the wave bears farther and farther from me."

How, after so much illumination, he came to publish the story, how it was that his friends did not combine to dissuade him, seems hard to understand. He had already, in an essay on "Great and little Things," published in the New Monthly Magazine early in 1822 (and reprinted in " Table Talk"), committed himself by a rhapsodical reference to his " Infelice" dragged in head and shoulders. Mrs. Hazlitt refers to the indiscretion in her diary for July 17th. " I told him," she writes, "he had done a most injudicious thing publishing what he did in the Magazine about Sarah Walker, particularly at this time, and that he might be sure it would be made use of against him, and that everybody in London had thought it a most improper thing, and Mr. John Hunt was quite sorry that he had so committed himself." I have quoted the passage in question in a note to Mrs. Hazlitt's Journal, pp. lxx.—lxxiv.

John Hunt's regret at the indiscretion seems to have been short-lived, for it did not prevent his publishing the still greater indiscretion of the " Liber Amoris," within a few months afterwards. Though Hunt published it, Mr. C. H. Reynell was, for £100, the purchaser of the copyright. Was it that Hazlitt had one of his periodical fits of impecuniosity on him, and could not resist this opportunity of coining his heart in guineas ?   However it happened, a man could hardly have done a more deliberately stupid injury to his fame. He had thus freely given his " Blackwood's" enemies an opportunity for which they had thirsted for years, and for which they would have gladly paid any price.   And you may be sure they did not miss the opportunity.   He was no longer to be "pimpled Hazlitt," but "the new Pygmalion!"

In the number for June, 1823, appeared a long review in their most cut-throat style, garnished with long quotations of the most outspoken passages, which lost none of their piquancy by the aid of copious capitals and italics. As this seems a more than usually interesting "cobweb of criticism," I venture to make a somewhat lengthy extract.

After some preliminary banter, the reviewer thus settles down to his scalping in real earnest:—

"To be serious:—we have long wished that some of this precious brotherhood would embody in a plain English narrative, concerning plain English transactions, the ideas of their school concerning morality, and the plain household relations of society. We now have our wish; and it is certainly not the less desirably accomplished, because the work is not a novel, but a history; not a creation of mere Cockney imagination, but a *veritable* transcript of the feelings and doings of an individual living LIBERAL. We shall make a few extracts, and leave our readers to form their opinion of this H——."

"The following fragments are extracted from the correspondence of our romantic H——, who, it will be seen, is an active gentleman of the press, and writes lustily at the rate of five pounds odd a sheet (for the *Liberal?* or the *Examiner?*) in the midst of his calamities."

The reviewer then proceeds to extract
some of those passages referring to what
Sarah Walker described as "liberties"—not
forgetting to draw eloquent attention to the
reference to "Endymion"—also the conversation between Hazlitt and her father (see
pp. 137—142) which, somewhat incompre-
hensibly, winds him up to a perfect moral
fury:

"'Would she have me, or would she not?' HE
SAID HE COULD NOT TELL.

Reader, this scene passes between H—— and *the
father of the young woman he wishes to make his
wife!* What delicacy! what manliness! what a veil
is here rent away! what abomination is disclosed!
What, after this, is a COCKNEY and A LIBERAL?'"

Then in his most impressive manner:

"Good public, since we first took pen in hand, nothing
so disgusting as this has ever fallen in our way. We
have gone through with it, because we conceived that
not to do so would be a most serious breach of public
duty in a journal which may trace five-sixths of all
the vulgar abuse that has been heaped upon its
character and conduct to this one single fact, that
IT HAS EXPOSED AND RUINED THE COCKNEY
SCHOOL. So long as examples were to be drawn

from Italianized poetasterisms, and unintelligible
essays, it might be that some should hesitate about
adopting *all* our conclusions.   We now bid them
farewell : we now leave them for once and for ever in
the hands of every single individual, however humble
in station, however limited in knowledge and acquire-
ment, who has elevation enough to form the least
notion of what 'virtue,' 'honour' and 'manliness,'
and, we may add, 'love,' mean—and penetration
enough to understand a plain English story told in
plain English.

This book is printed for the same JOHN HUNT
who is the publisher of the *Liberal* and the *Examiner*,
and the brother of Leigh Hunt, the author of
'Rimini,' and the 'Letters from Abroad.'   The
elegant, polite, chivalrous, pure, high-spirited, five-
guinea-per-sheet gentleman of the press, who writes
this book, and tells this story, is a fair specimen of the
tribe of authors to which he belongs (at this moment
they are all busy in puffing him as a new Rousseau),
and he speaks in the course of his work elegantly,
kindly, and familiarly, of 'CRAIGCROOK, WHERE
LIVES THE FIRST OF CRITICS, AND THE KING OF
MEN.'   So then it seems H—— is a friend of
Mr. Jeffrey's !—well, we wish Mr. H—— much joy
of the acquaintance—but no—we correct ourselves—
Mr. Jeffrey could not *then* have known the story of
'Sally in our Alley !' and Mr. H—— will not
speedily nestle again at Craigcrook ! "

We leave ' H——' in the hands not of the ' First

of Critics and the King of Men,' but of the British public; and we call down upon his head, and upon the heads of those accomplished reformers in ethics, religion and politics, who are now enjoying his *chef d'œuvre*, the scorn and loathing of every thing that bears the name of MAN. Woman!—But it would be insult to go farther."

It will no doubt interest the reader to know what "those accomplished reformers in ethics, &c.," actually had to say of the "Liber Amoris." The *Blackwoodsman* evidently refers to a review which had appeared in the *Examiner* of May 11th. It is a sly and witty piece of writing, and one still smiles at the way in which the critic, while assuming with much seriousness that the author was dead, as stated in the advertisement, keeps significantly referring to "the unhappy person deceased in the Netherlands," "the gentleman who died in the Netherlands"—as with an "ahem!" in the voice. The reader, too, will notice the clever application of the Berkeleyan theory:

"The lover, the poet, and another sort of person, we are told by Shakespeare," begins 'the Examiner' reviewer:—

" ' Are of imagination all compact ; '

and if so, singly considered, what must be the state
of the case when two or more of them are united in
the same person ? In the common acceptation of
the term, we have no evidence to prove that the
St. Preux of this little book is a poet, but in its
higher and more enlarged sense he is clearly so ; and
admitting the two former characteristics to be self-
existent, and the last ' proceeding,' we have an
exemplification of the imaginative trio of Shakespeare in the single author of *Liber Amoris*. We are
not aware indeed of the publication of anything so
indicative of the Ideal theory of Bishop Berkeley,
since the publication of ' The Academical Questions '
of Sir William Drummond—nothing so approaching
to a demonstration that mind is the great creator,
and matter a fable. . . . Its essence consists in
the eloquence of soul and of passion which these
trite and by no means exalted events indicate. Whatever Werter may be in the original garb of Göethe,
we have always thought him a somewhat spiritless
personage in his English dress ; but whether this be
so or no, the incident of that German production
is by no means of the first order. The St. Preux of
Rousseau is a very different creation, and with a
somewhat stronger breathing of physical ardour—
l'amour physique, as Gil Blas calls it—the gentleman who died in the Netherlands in some degree
resembles him. . . .

We regret exceedingly the death of the impassioned
author, because we are of opinion, from the close of
the book, that if he had lived for some time longer
he would have survived his passion. . . .

At all events, 'Liber Amoris' is a novelty in the
English language, and we doubt not will be received
as a *rara avis* in this land of phlegm and sea-coal."

The modern reader will hardly take the
"Liber Amoris" as seriously as either of these
critics. It will not on the one hand seem so
dangerously immoral, or on the other so
finely artistic a piece of work here at the
end as it did there at the beginning of the
century. Perhaps that highly proper *Blackwoodsman* was not really quite so shocked as
he felt it necessary to appear. More recent
examples have proved that the sins of one's
political adversaries are as scarlet. Far from
taking so grave a view of Hazlitt's amour, we
are more likely to see in the very violence of
the aberration a witness to the essential
innocence of his nature at the time. It seems
to say that, despite those confidences with
Patmore and others at "The Southampton,"
Hazlitt's life had actually been freer from
taint than the lives of most men. Few men

of his years remain capable of taking any woman so seriously, not to speak of a little servant-girl. Possibly Sarah Walker's station —a serving-maid, "out of thy star"—will seem the least forgivable part of the affair to certain natures, to whom the charm of print-stuff, save in the authorised forms of blouse or boating costume, has not been revealed. Some will perhaps be able to forgive Hazlitt all the easier on that account. Cophetua's was a true story. For Hazlitt, the reader must make sure not to forget, meant honour-ably by his beggar-maid. It is a pity his assurances of those honourable intentions make such ludicrous reading. Indeed, the one sin which we find in his book to-day is the sin against humour. Though, as we have said, the illusion did credit to Hazlitt's heart, it is impossible not to feel that no man of forty should be able to mistake a woman for a goddess or an angel, and he should certainly never quote Milton or any good poet to her. It is unnatural, uncanny, in the bearded man. Naïveté is charming up to twenty, but the naïveté of middle-age

is unattractive, and the "Liber Amoris" is
full of that unattractive quality,—much like
the naïveté we sometimes find in the poetical
effusions of criminals.

To think of poor Hazlitt gravely lavishing
his choice Elizabethan quotations on the
hussey, not sparing even to lay at her feet
his sacred passion for Napoleon! Was ever
in the history of amorous sentiment anything more ludicrous than the tiresome
nonsense about "the little image"! There
is indeed, as Hazlitt himself says, something
in it all "discordant to honest ears."

Viewed as literature, it is impossible to
agree with the reviewer in "The Examiner"
that "the gentleman who died in the Netherlands" is worthy to be mentioned in the
same day as Rousseau. Remembering Hazlitt's devotion to *The New Héloïse*, it seems
strange that he should not have succeeded
better. The reader will remember how he
used to carry it in his pocket during his
walking-tours, and will recall especially that
passage where he tells us: "It was on the
10th of April, 1798, that I sat down to a

volume of the New *Eloïse*, at the Inn at
Llangollen, over a bottle of sherry and a cold
chicken." It is not inappropriate that we have
thus recalled that other robuster Hazlitt, who
in his other writings, so full of bracing manliness, seems so little related to the maudlin
sentimentalist of the book before us. Un-
likely as it seems, should any reader encounter
this book who has not previously made
Hazlitt's acquaintance, I must beg him
in justice to a fine writer to acquire his
other books at once. To those who know
the Hazlitt of the glorious essays "On
Going a Journey," "My First Acquaintance
with Poets," "On the Fear of Death," the
"Liber Amoris" may be entrusted without
fear. They will know where to place it, in
a very subsidiary relation indeed to the
Hazlitt beloved of Mr. Stevenson and all
honest men who love virile English. It is
but as a literary curiosity, a document of
nympholepsy, a biographical appendix, that
the "Liber Amoris" has any value—unless
one sees in the literal tone of its opening
conversations a näive promise of modern

realism, a prophecy of Mr. George Moore.

Properly speaking, it is necessary to the understanding of Hazlitt's curious disposition. Many critics now-a-days advocate doctored biography. In view of a public which is far too inclined to magnify all the warts of its great men, there is, doubtless, something to be said for such a theory. Truth of presentation, under the most favourable circumstances, is so hopeless a quest, that we might as well, perhaps, frankly regard biography as a form of fiction, founded upon fact. But, so long as we keep up the pretence of truth-telling, I cannot see how we can logically hush up any side of our great men. It is only a very childish, incomplete view of human nature that would ask it. Surely a great man hangs together like any other organism, and to ignore any one element in him is to stultify the rest. To pretend to know Hazlitt and to ignore the "Liber Amoris" is, in a less degree, as though you should write a life of Coleridge and never even whisper "opium." But, whereas Coleridge's weakness was disastrous, Hazlitt's was only silly. It did no one any harm but himself.

RICHARD LE GALLIENNE.

———

NOTE.—*In the following reprint of the* " Liber Amoris " *the text of the original edition* (1823) *has been scrupulously followed. There has been but one other reprint, that in the* " Bibliotheca Curiosa " [? 1884]. *My best thanks are due: to Mr. W. C. Hazlitt for his kindness in allowing me to print the extrac t from Mr. Hazlitt's diary, and to make other use of his* "Memoirs" *of his illustrious grandfather ; also to Mr. Coventry Patmore for a similar permission in the case of Mr. P. G. Patmore's* "My Friends and Acquaintance " ; *also to Mr. Alexander Ireland and Mr. William Watson for one or two references. Among the few accounts of the* "Liber Amoris," *I desire to mention a pleasant paper in an old* "Fraser," *which, I understand, was written by Mr. Ashcroft Noble.*

APPENDICES.

APPENDIX I.

Sunday, 21st [April].—At 5 a.m. calm. At 1 p.m.
landed safe at Leith. A laddie brought my luggage
with me to the Black Bull, Catherine Street,
Edinburgh. Dined at three on mutton chops. Met
Mr. Bell at the door, as I was going to take a walk
after dinner. He had been on board the vessel to
inquire for me. After he went, I walked up to Edinburgh. . . . Returned to tea. . . . Went
to bed at half-past twelve.

Monday, 22nd [April]. . . . Mr. Bell called
about twelve, and I went with him to Mr. Cranstoun,
the barrister, to consult him on the practicability and
safety of procuring a divorce, and informed him that
my friends in England had rather alarmed me by
asserting that, if I took the oath of calumny, and
swore that there was no collusion between Mr. Hazlitt
and myself to procure the divorce, I should be liable
to a prosecution and transportation for perjury. Mr.
Hazlitt having certainly told me that he should never
live with me again, and as my situation must have
long been uncomfortable, he thought for both our
sakes it would be better to obtain a divorce, and put
an end to it. . . . .

Tuesday 23rd.—Consulted Mr. Gray [a solicitor].
. . . . . The case must be submitted to the
procurators to decide whether I may be admitted to
the oath of calumny. If they agree to it, the oath
to be administered, then Mr. Hazlitt to be cited in
answer to the charge, and if not defended [I told
him I was sure Mr. Hazlitt had no such intention, as
he was quite as desirous of obtaining the divorce as
me], he said then, if no demur or difficulty arose
about proofs, the cause would probably occupy two
months, and cost £50, but that I should have to send
to England for the testimony of two witnesses who
were present at the marriage, and also to testify that
we acknowledged each other as husband and wife,
and were so esteemed by our friends, neighbours,
acquaintances, &c. He said it was fortunate that
Mr. and Mrs. Bell were here to bear testimony to the
latter part. And that I must also procure a certificate of my marriage from St. Andrew's Church,
Holborn. I took the questions which Mr. Gray
wrote . . . . . to Mr. Bell, who added a note,
and I put it in the penny post. Sent also the paper
signed by Mr. Hazlitt securing the reversion of my
money to the child, which Mr. Bell had given me, by
the mail to Coulson, requesting him to get it properly
stamped and return it to me, together with the certificate of my marriage. . . . .

Thursday, 25th April [1822].—Mr. Bell called to
ask if he could be of any assistance to me. I had
just sent a note to Mr. Hazlitt to say that I demurred

to the oath, so there was no occasion to trouble Mr.
Bell. In the afternoon Mr. Ritchie, of the *Scotsman*
newspaper, called to beg me, as a friend to both (I
had never seen or heard of him before), to proceed in
the divorce, and relieve all parties from an unpleasant
situation. Said that with my appearance it was
highly probable that I might marry again, and meet
with a person more congenial to me than Mr. Hazlitt
had unfortunately proved. That Mr. Hazlitt was in
such a state of nervous irritability that he could not
work or apply to anything, and that he thought that
he would not live very long if he was not easier in
his mind. I told him I did not myself think that he
would survive me. . . . . In the evening Mr.
Bell called. . . . . I then told him of Mr.
Ritchie's visit, at which he seemed much surprised,
and said if Mr. Hazlitt had sent him, as I supposed,
he acted with great want of judgment and prudence.
. . . .

Saturday, 27th April.—Gave Mr. Bell the stamp
for the 50*l.* bill, and the following paper of memo-
randum for Mr. Hazlitt to sign :—

" 1. William Hazlitt to pay the whole expense of
board, clothing, and education, for his son, William
Hazlitt, by his wife, Sarah Hazlitt (late Stoddart),
and she to be allowed free access to him at all times,
and occasional visits from him.

" 2. William Hazlitt to pay board, lodging, law,
and all other expenses incurred by his said wife
during her stay in Scotland on this divorce business,

together with travelling expenses.

"3. William Hazlitt to give a note-of-hand for fifty pounds at six months, payable to William Netherfold or order. Value Received."

Mr. Bell said he would go that day to Mr. Gray . . . . . then go on to Mr. Hazlitt's, and call on me afterwards; but I saw no more of him.

Sunday, 28th April, 1822.—Wrote to Mr. Hazlitt to inform him I had only between five and six pounds of my quarter's money left, and therefore, if he did not send me some immediately, and fulfil his agreement for the rest, I should be obliged to return on Tuesday, while I had enough to take me back. Sent the letter by a laddie. Called on Mr. Bell, who said that Mr. Gray was not at home when he called, but that he had seen his son, and appointed to be with him at ten o'clock on Monday morning. Told him that Mr. Hazlitt said he would give the draft to fifty pounds at three months instead of six, when the proceedings had commenced (meaning, I suppose, when the oath was taken, for they had already commenced) but would do nothing before. Told me he was gone to Lanark, but would be back on Monday morning.

. . . . . .

Tuesday, 30th April.—Went to Mr. Bell after dinner, who did not know whether Mr. Hazlitt was returned or not. . . . . In the evening, after some hesitation, went to Mr. Hazlitt myself for an answer. He told me he expected thirty pounds from Colburn on Thursday, and then he would let me have five pounds for present expenses; that he had but one pound in his pocket, but if I wanted it, I should have that. That he was going to give two lectures at Glasgow next week, for which he was to have 100*l.*, and he had eighty pounds beside to receive for the 'Table Talk' in a fortnight, out of which sums he pledged himself to fulfil his engagements relative to my expenses : and also to make me a handsome present, when it was over (20*l.*), as I seemed to love money. Or it would enable me to travel back by land, as I said I should prefer seeing something of the country to going back in the steamboat, which he proposed. Said he would give the note-of-hand for fifty pounds to Mr. Ritchie for me, payable to whoever I pleased : if he could conveniently at the time, it should be for three months instead of six, but he was not certain of that. . . . Inquired if I had taken the oath. I told him I only waited a summons from Mr. Gray, if I could depend upon the money, but I could not live in a strange place without : and I had no friends or means of earning money here as he had ; though as I had still four pounds, I could wait a few days. I asked him how the expenses, or my draught, were to be paid, if he went abroad, and he answered that, if he succeeded in the divorce, he should be easy in his mind, and able to work, and then he should probably be back in three months ; but otherwise, he might leave England for ever. He said that as soon as I had got him to sign a paper giving away a 150*l.* a year from

himself, I talked of going back, and leaving everything. . . . . I told him to recollect that it was
no advantage for myself that I sought . . . . it
was only to secure something to *his* child as well as
mine. He said he could do very well for the child
himself; and that he was allowed to be a very indulgent, kind father—some people thought too much so.
I said I did not dispute his fondness for him, but I
must observe that though he got a great deal of
money, he never saved or had any by him, or was
likely to make much provision for the child ; neither
could I think it was proper, or for his welfare that he
should take him to the Fives Court, and such places
. . . . it was likely to corrupt and vitiate him.
. . . . He said perhaps it was wrong, but that
he did not know that it was any good to bring up
children in ignorance of the world. . . . . He
said I had always despised him and his abilities.
. . . . He said that a paper had been brought to
him from Mr. Gray that day, but that he was only
just come in from Lanark, after walking thirty miles,
and was getting his tea. . . . .

Thursday, 2nd May [1822].—-Mr. Bell called to say
Mr. Hazlitt would sign the papers to-morrow and
leave [them] in his hand. And that he should bring
me the first five pounds. When he was gone, I
wrote to Mr. Hazlitt, requesting him to leave the
papers in Mr. Ritchie's hands, as he had before proposed.

Friday, 3rd May.—Received the certificate of my

marriage, and the stamped paper transferring my money to the child after my death, from Coulson, the carriage of which cost seven shillings. Called on Mr. Gray, who said, on my asking him when my presence would be necessary in the business, that he should not call on me till this day three weeks. . . . .

Saturday, 4th May, 1822. — Mr. Ritchie called, and gave me 4*l.*, said Mr. Hazlitt could not spare more then, as he was just setting off for Glasgow. . . . .

Tuesday, 7th May.—Wrote to my little son. . .

Tuesday, 21st May. — Wrote to Mr. Hazlitt for money. The note was returned with a message that he was gone to London, and would not be back for a fortnight.

Wednesday, 22nd. — Called on Mr. Ritchie to inquire what I was to do for money, as Mr. Hazlitt had gone off without sending me any : he seemed surprised to hear he was in London, but conjectured he was gone about the publication of his book, took his address, and said he would write to him in the evening.

Sunday, 9th June, 1822.—Sent a letter to Mr. Hazlitt to remit the money he had promised.

Monday, 10th June.— . . . . Received a note from Mr. Ritchie, to say he would come the next day and explain about money matters to me. Had also a letter from the child. . . . .

Tuesday, 11th June.— . . . . . Mr. Ritchie

came. . . . .   Told me that Mr. Hazlitt only
got 56*l.* from Glasgow, and nothing from Colburn,
so that he could not give me the money I asked, but
that he had told him whatever small sums of money
I wanted to go on with, he would let me have by
some means or other.

Thursday, 13*th June* [1822]. — Mr. Bell called,
and said that Mr. Hazlitt had gone to Renton Inn,
but that he would remit me some money, which he
showed him he had for the purpose, as soon as the
oath was taken, which he said he was to give him
due notice of. . . . .   Asked if I did not take
the oath to-morrow ?   I said I had not heard from
Mr. Gray, but was in hourly expectation of it. . . .
The note came soon after, appointing the next day.
. . . .

Friday, 14*th June.*—Mr. Bell called, and said he
was going to Mr. Gray's, and would come back for
me.   Returned, and said Mr. Gray informed him he
could not be admitted, as he would be called on with
Mrs. Bell the next Friday as witnesses.   So I undertook to let him know when the ceremony was over.
[Here follows the description of the taking of the
oath.] . . . .   On the whole, with the utmost
expedition they can use, and supposing no impedi-
ments, it will be five weeks from this day before all is
finished.   Went down and reported this to Mr. and
Mrs. Bell : dined there.   They told me that Mr.
Hazlitt took 90*l.* to the Renton Inn with him. . . .
Mr. Bell undertook to send him a parcel that night

with the joyful intelligence of the oath being taken,
as he would get it sooner that way than by the post.
. . . .

Saturday, 15*th June.*—Mr. Bell called, and wrote
a letter to Mr. Hazlitt here, and made it into a
parcel, not having sent to him last night, as he
promised. Wrote to Peggy. Feel very faint to-day.

Sunday, 16*th June* [1822].— . . . . Adam
Bell called, while I was at breakfast, to say that Mr.
Hazlitt was come back, and had been at their house
the night before. . . . .

Monday, 17*th June.*—Went to Mr. Bell as soon
as I had breakfasted. He told me that Mr. Ritchie
was to bring me 20*l.* that day in part of payment,
and that the rest would he paid me as Mr. Hazlitt
could get it. That he had proposed only ten now,
but that Mr. Bell had told him that *that* would not
do, as I proposed taking some journey, and had no
money. Said he did not know anything about the
child. Went home very uneasy about him, as his
holidays were to begin this day ; and I fretted that
he should be left there, and thought he would be
very uneasy if they had not sent him to Winterslow,
and feel quite unhappy and forsaken ; and thought
on his father's refusing to tell me where he was to
be, till I was so nervous and hysterical I could not
stay in the house.

Went down to Mr. Bell's again at one, as they
told me he [Mr. H.] would be there about that time,
that I might see him myself, and know where the

child was. He was not come, and Mr. Bell did not like my meeting him there. I told him if I could not gain information of the child, I would set off to London directly, and find him out, and leave the business here just as it was. He then gave me a note to send him [Mr. H.] about it, but I carried it myself, and asked to see him.

They said he was out, but would return at three o'clock. I left the note, and went at three. They then said he would be back to dinner at four. I wandered about between that and Mr. Bell's till four; then, going again, I met him by the way: he gave me 10*l.*, and said I should have more soon by Mr. Bell. I said I did not like Mr. Bell; I had rather he sent by Mr. Ritchie, which he said he would.

I asked about the child, and he said he was going to write that night to Mr. John Hunt about him; so that the poor little fellow is really fretting, and thinking himself neglected. . . . .

Mr. Bell said that he seemed quite enamoured of a letter he had been writing to Patmore; that in their walk the day before he pulled it out of his pocket twenty times, and wanted to read it to them; that he talked so loud, and acted so extravagantly, that the people stood and stared at them as they passed, and seemed to take him for a madman. . .

[The next twelve days were spent by Mrs. H. in the tour to the Highlands and to Dublin. She returned on the 28th June.]

Saturday, 29th June, 1822. — Sent the child's letter to his father with a note, telling him that I was just returned from Dublin with four shillings and sixpence in my pocket, and I wanted more money. He came about two o'clock, and brought me ten pounds, and said he did not think he was indebted to me my quarter's money, as he had supplied me with more than was necessary to keep me. . . . . He had been uneasy at not hearing from the child, though he had sent him a pound and ordered him to write. I remarked that the letter I sent him was addressed to him, and I supposed the child did not know how to direct to him. He said he would if he had attended to what he told him. That he wrote to Patmore, and desired him to see for the child, and convey him to Mr. John Hunt's, and that in his answer he said, "I have been to the school, and rejoiced the poor little fellow's heart by bringing him away with me, and in the afternoon he is going by the stage to Mr. Hunt's* He has only been detained two days after the holidays begun." . . . That Mr. Prentice had told him last night it [the business] was again put off another fortnight; requested me to write to Mr. Gray, to know whether I should be called on next Friday, and if it would be necessary for me to remain in Scotland after that time; if not, he thought I had better go on the Saturday by the steamboat, as the accommodation was excellent, and

* At Taunton.

it was very pleasant and good company. That he intended going by it himself, as soon as he could, when the affair was over, and therefore I had better set out first, as our being seen there together would be awkward, and would look like making a mockery of the lawyers here. Wished I would also write to the child in the evening, as his nerves were in such an irritable state he was unable to do so. Both which requests I complied with.

Monday, 1st July. — Received a note from Mr. Gray, to say I should not be called on for two or three weeks, but without telling me how long I must remain in Scotland.

Saturday, 6th July [1822].—.　.　.　. Met Mr. Hazlitt and Mr. Henderson, who had just arrived [at Dalkeith Palace] in a gig. Mr. H. said he had heard again from Patmore, who saw the child last Tuesday, and that he was well and happy. I told him of my last letter and its contents. .　.　.　. [He] adverted again to the awkwardness of our going back in the same boat. I told him I had some thoughts of going by boat to Liverpool and the rest by land, as I should see more of the country that way ; which he seemed to like. Asked me if I meant to go to Winterslow ? Said, yes, but that I should be a week or two in London first. He said he meant to go to Winterslow, and try if he could write,* for he had been so distracted the last five months he could do nothing.

* Mrs. H. had a house in the village, but Mr. H. put up at the Hut. A strangely close juxtaposition!

That he might also go to his mother's† for a short
time, and that he meant to take the child from school
at the half-quarter, and take him with him; and that
after the holidays at Christmas he should return to
Mr. Dawson's again.   Said he had not been to town
[London], and that we had better have no communication at present, but that when it was over he would
let me have the money as he could get it.   Asked if
I had seen Roslin Castle, and said he was there last
Tuesday with Bell, and thought it a fine place.   Mr.
Henderson shook hands, and made many apologies
for not recollecting me, and said I looked very well,
but that from my speaking to Mr. H. about the
pictures, he had taken me for an artist. . . . .
The two gentlemen passed me in their gig as I was
returning.

Wednesday, 10*th* *July* [1822]. — Called on Mr.
Ritchie, to ask if he thought I should finish the
business on Monday ?   I told him that I wanted to
know what was to be done about my own payment,
as Mr. Hazlitt now seemed to demur to the one
quarter that he had all along agreed to, and there
was also the 20*l*. that I was to have as a present.   He
said that he was at present very much engaged in
some business which would end in two days more,
and that then, if I was at all apprehensive about it,
he would write to, or see, Mr. Hazlitt on the subject.

Thursday, 11*th* *July*. — Met   Mr. Hazlitt in

† At Alphington, near Exeter.

Catherine Street, and asked him what I was to do if
Mr. Gray sent in my bill to me, and he said I had
nothing to do with it, for that he had paid Mr.
Prentice 40*l.*, which was nearly the whole expense for
both of them. I said that was what Mr. Ritchie, to
whom I had spoken about it, thought. He said Mr.
Ritchie had nothing at all to do with it, and I
remarked that he was the person he had sent to me
about it, and that he did not think it would finish on
Monday; and [I] asked if he had heard anything
more ? He said no, but he thought it would be
Monday or Tuesday ; and as soon as it was done, he
wished I would come to him to finally settle matters,
as he had some things to say, and I told him I
would. I was rather flurried at meeting him, and
totally forgot many things I wished to have said,
which vexed me afterwards.

Friday, 12*th July*.—On my return [from a walk to
Holyrood House] I found a note from Mr. Gray,
appointing next Wednesday for my attendance, and
desiring a "payment of 20*l*. towards the expense."
I took it to Mr. Bell's ; he and Mr. Hazlitt went out
at the back door as I went in at the front. I gave
the message to Mrs. Bell, who told me Mr. Hazlitt
had been to Mr. Gray's. . . . .

Saturday, 13*th July*.—Met Mr. Hazlitt at the foot
of my stairs, coming to me. He said that Mr. Gray
was to have the money out of what he had paid Mr.
Prentice. . . . . I told him he need not be
uneasy about meeting me in the steamboat, for I did

not intend to go that way. Asked him if he thought
it a good collection of pictures at Dalkeith House
[this is so characteristic!]; he said no, very poor.
. . . .

Wednesday, 17*th July.*—Mr. Bell called between
ten and eleven. . . . . He had come, by Mr.
Gray's desire, to accompany me to the court, and was
himself cited as a witness. [Mrs. H. then describes
going to the court, but the proceedings were *pro
formâ,* as the depositions had been arranged to be
taken at Mr. Bell's private residence.] Returned,
and wrote a note to Mr. Hazlitt, to have in case he
was out, saying that I would call on him at two
o'clock. I left it. . . . . Saw Mr. Hazlitt at
four o'clock; he was at dinner; but I stopped and
drank tea with him. [!] He told me that all was
done now, unless Mrs. Bell should make any demur
in the part required of her. . . . . Said he
would set off to London by the mail that night,
though he thought he should be detained by illness
or die on the road, for he had been penned up in that
house for five months . . . . unable to do any
work; and he thought he had lost the job to Italy,
but to get out of Scotland would seem like the road
to Paradise. *I told him* he had done a most in-*

---

* The italics are mine. This passage must find room here,
in spite of my scruples. The affair was well known, and was
soon in print in the 'Liber Amoris.' To conceal it would be
useless; and all that I can do is to place it in its true light
before the world. Mrs. H. was a plain - spoken woman,
without any false delicacy about her. She was perfectly
acquainted with the whole history of the matter.—[*Mr. W.
C. Hazlitt's note.*]

judicious thing in publishing what he did in the [New Monthly] *Magazine about Sarah Walker, particularly at this time, and that he might be sure it would be made use of against him, and that everybody in London had thought it a most improper thing, and Mr. John Hunt was quite sorry that he had so committed himself.**

He said that *he* was sorry for [it], but that it was done *without his knowledge or consent*. That Colburn had got hold of it by mistake, with other papers, *and published it without sending him the proofs*. He asked me where I should be in town, and I told him at Christie's. He inquired what kind of people they were. I told him a very respectable quiet young couple lately married. He desired me to take care of myself, and keep up a respectable appearance, as I had money enough to do so. *He† wished he could marry some woman with a good fortune, that he might not be under the necessity of writing another line ; and be enabled to provide for the child, and do something for John ; and that now his name was known in the literary world, he thought there was a chance for it, though he could not pretend to anything of the kind before.* . . . . I left Mr. Henderson with him, pressing him to accompany him to the Highlands ; but he seemed, after some hesita-

* See note at end.

† The italics are mine. The *John* referred to presently was, of course, his brother. This passage is very remarkable. —[*Mr. W. C. Hazlitt's note.*]

tion, to prefer going to London, though I left the
matter uncertain. He [Mr. Henderson] had been
dawdling backward and forward about it for three
weeks, wishing to have the credit of taking him
there, but grudging the money, though he was living
upon us for a week together in London.

Mr. Hazlitt said that, if he went to Winterslow, he
would take the child, as he wished to have him a
little with him ; so I thought he had better go with
the first that went, as I did not think of staying in
town more than two or three weeks, and then making
some stay at Winterslow, and proceeding afterwards
to Crediton.* He said we could settle that best in
town.

Mrs. Dow [Mr. H.'s landlady] brought in the bill,
which he just looked at and said, " Is that the
whole, ma'am ? " " Yes, sir ; you had better look
over it, and see that it is correct, if you please."
" *That*, ma'am," he said, " is one of the troubles I
get rid of. I never do it." " You are a very indolent
man, sir." " There is a balance of twenty-four
shillings, ma'am ; can you have so much confidence
in me as to let me have that ? " " No, sir, I can't do
that, for I have not the money." " I shall be glad
then, ma'am, if you will let me have the four
shillings, and you may pay the pound to Mrs. Hazlitt

* Where Mr. H.'s relations were settled ! This is also a
curious part of the business. My grandmother was intimate
and friendly with the Hazlitts to the last, and frequently
visited them here.—[*Mr. W. C. Hazlitt's note.*]

on Saturday, as when it comes, she will be here."
"Yes, sir, and Mrs. Hazlitt may look over the bill, if
she pleases."

Thursday, 18th July [1822].—She returned with
the four shillings, saying she had been to two or
three places to get that. . . . . Went to Mr.
Ritchie, who gave me the note-of-hand for fifty
pounds at six months, dated 6th May, and the copy
of memorandums signed by Mr. Hazlitt. . . . .
He said he had expected him and Mr. Henderson to
supper last night, but they did not come. I told
him he wished to go to London by the mail, and
probably had done so. . . . . He said he must
repeat that he thought we had taken the step most
advisable for both parties. . . . . Called at his
[Mr. H.'s] lodgings to inquire if he went by the mail.
Mrs. Dow said yes; he left there about eight o'clock.
. . . . Called at the coach-office, and they said
Mr. Hazlitt did not go by the mail. Saw the waiter
at the inn door, who said he went by the steamboat
at eight o'clock this morning. . . . .

Carried back Mrs. Bell's book. Mr. Bell said I
was a great fool to have acceded to his wish for a
divorce, but that it was now done, and he thought I
had better get some old rich Scotch lord, and marry
here. "I was now Miss Stoddart, and was I not
glad of that?" "No; I had no intention of marrying, and should not do what he talked of." He said
I must needs marry; and I told him I saw no such
necessity. . . . ."

This is the conclusion.   Mrs. Hazlitt sailed on the
following day, at 2 p.m., in the smack *Favourite*
from Leith.

PASSAGE IN ESSAY "ON GREAT AND LITTLE
THINGS" (WRITTEN JANUARY, 1821, PRINTED IN
NEW MONTHLY MAGAZINE, N.S. VOL. IV. 1822;
AND REPRINTED IN "TABLE TALK") REFERRED
TO IN MRS. HAZLITT'S DIARY, PP. LXV. AND LXVI.

"This is the misery of unequal matches. The woman
cannot easily forget, or think that others forget, her
origin; and with perhaps superior sense and beauty,
keeps painfully in the back-ground. It is worse
when she braves this conscious feeling, and displays
all the insolence of the upstart and affected fine lady.
But shouldst thou ever, my Infelice, grace my home
with thy loved presence, as thou hast cheered my
hopes with thy smile, thou wilt conquer all hearts
with thy prevailing gentleness, and I will show the
world what Shakespear's women were!—Some
gallants set their hearts on princesses; others descend
in imagination to women of quality; others are mad
after opera-singers. For my part, I am shy even of
actresses, and should not think of leaving my card
with Madame Vestris. I am for none of these *bonnes
fortunes*; but for a list of humble beauties, servant-
maids and shepherd-girls, with their red elbows, hard

hands, black stockings and mob-caps, I could furnish
out a gallery equal to Cowley's, and paint them half
as well. Oh! might I but attempt a description of
some of them in poetic prose, Don Juan would forget
his Julia, and Mr. Davison might both print and
publish this volume. I agree so far with Horace, and
differ with Montaigne. I admire the Clementinas
and Clarissas at a distance : the Pamelas and Fannys
of Richardson and Fielding make my blood tingle.
I have written love-letters to such in my time, *d'un
pathetique à faire fendre les rochers*, and with about
as much effect as if they had been addressed to
stone. The simpletons only laughed, and said, that
" those were not the sort of things to gain the
affections." I wish I had kept copies in my own
justification. What is worse, I have an utter aversion
to *blue stockings*. I do not care a fig for any woman
that knows even what *an author* means. If I know
that she has read anything I have written, I cut her
acquaintance immediately. This sort of literary intercourse with me passes for nothing. Her critical and
scientific acquirements are *carrying coals to New-
castle*. I do not want to be told that I have published
such or such a work. I knew all this before. It
makes no addition to my sense of power. I do not
wish the affair to be brought about in that way. I
would have her read my soul : she should understand
the language of the heart : she should know what I
am, as if she were another self ! She should love me
for myself alone. I like myself without any reason :

I would have her do so too. This is not very reason-
able. I abstract from my temptations to admire all
the circumstances of dress, birth, breeding, fortune;
and I would not willingly put forward my own pretensions, whatever they may be. The image of some
fair creature is engraven on my inmost soul; it is on
that I build my claim to her regard, and expect her to
see into my heart, as I see her form always before me.
Wherever she treads, pale primroses, like her face,
vernal hyacinths, like her brow, spring up beneath her
feet, and music hangs on every bough : but all is cold,
barren, and desolate without her. Thus I feel, and
thus I think. But have I ever told her so ? No. Or
if I did, would she understand it ? No. I " hunt the
wind, I worship a statue, cry aloud to the desert."
To see beauty is not to be beautiful, to pine in love is
not to be loved again.—I always was inclined to raise
and magnify the power of Love. I thought that his
sweet power should only be exerted to join together
the loveliest forms and fondest hearts; that none but
those in whom his godhead shone outwardly, and was
inly felt, should ever partake of his triumphs; and I
stood and gazed at a distance, as unworthy to mingle
in so bright a throng, and did not (even for a moment)
wish to tarnish the glory of so fair a vision by being
myself admitted into it. I say this was my notion
once, but God knows it was one of the errors of my
youth. For coming nearer to look, I saw the maimed,
the blind, and the halt enter in, the crooked and the
dwarf, the ugly, the old and impotent, the man of

pleasure and the man of the world, the dapper and the
pert, the vain and shallow boaster, the fool and the
pedant, the ignorant and brutal, and all that is farthest
removed from earth's fairest-born, and the pride of
human life. Seeing all these enter the courts of Love,
and thinking that I also might venture in under favour
of the crowd, but finding myself rejected, I fancied
(I might be wrong) that it was not so much because I
was below, as above the common standard. I did
feel, but I was ashamed to feel, mortified at my repulse,
when I saw the meanest of mankind, the very scum
and refuse, all creeping things and every obscene
creature, enter in before me. I seemed a species by
myself. I took a pride even in my disgrace: and
concluded I had elsewhere my inheritance! The only
thing I ever piqued myself upon was the writing the
"Essay on the Principles of Human Action"*—a work
that no woman ever read, or would ever comprehend
the meaning of. But if I do not build my claim to
regard on the pretensions I have, how can I build it
on those I am totally without ? Or why do I complain
and expect to gather grapes of thorns, or figs of
thistles ? Thought has in me cancelled pleasure ; and
this dark forehead, bent upon truth, is the rock on
which all affection has split. And thus I waste my
life in one long sigh ; nor ever (till too late) beheld a
gentle face turned gently upon mine ;.... But no! not

* Published in 1805, but the composition of the work, though
a thin octavo, cost the author seven or eight years' labour.—
[ED.]

too late, if that face, pure, modest, downcast, tender,
with angel sweetness, not only gladdens the prospect
of the future, but sheds its radiance on the past,
smiling in tears.   A purple light hovers round my
head.   The air of love is in the room.   As I look at
my long-neglected copy of the Death of Clorinda,*
golden gleams play upon the canvas, as they used
when I painted it.   The flowers of Hope and Joy
springing up in my mind, recal the time when they
first bloomed there.   The years that are fled knock at
the door and enter.   I am in the Louvre once more.
The sun of Austerlitz has not set.   It still shines
here—in my heart ; and he, the son of glory, is not
dead, nor ever shall, to me.   I am as when my life
began.   The rainbow is in the sky again.   I see the
skirts of the departed years.   All that I have thought
and felt has not been in vain.   I am not utterly
worthless, unregarded ;   nor shall I die and wither of
pure scorn.   Now could I sit on the tomb of Liberty,
and write a Hymn to Love.   Oh! if I am deceived,
let me be deceived still.   Let me live in the Elysium
of those soft looks ; poison me with kisses, kill me
with smiles ; but still mock me with thy love ! †

*. By Lana, Titian's contemporary.   It was copied by the
writer in 1802, and is still in good preservation.—[ED.]

† I beg the reader to consider this passage merely as a
specimen of the mock-heroic style, and as having nothing to
do with any real facts or feelings.

APPENDIX II.

"What have I suffered since I parted with you! A raging fire in my heart and in my brain, that I thought would drive me mad. The steam-boat seemed a prison—a hell—and the everlasting waters an unendurable repetition of the same idea—my woes. The abyss was before me, and *her* face, where all my peace was centred—all lost! I felt the eternity of punishment in this world. Mocked, mocked by her in whom I placed my hope—writhing, withering in misery and despair, caused by one who hardens herself against me. I wished for courage to throw myself into the waters; but I could not even do that —and my little boy, too, prevented me, when I thought of his face at hearing of his father's death, and his desolation in life.

*   *   *   *   *   *

"You see she all along hated me ('I always told you I had no affection for you'), and only played with me.

"I am a little, a very little, better to-day. Would it were quietly over, and that this form, made to be loathed, were hid out of sight of cold, sullen eyes. I thought of the breakfasts I had promised myself with her, of those I had had with her, standing and listening to my true vows; and compared them to the one I had this morning. The thought choked me. The people even take notice of my dumb despair, and pity me. What can be done? I cannot forget her, and I can find no other like *what she seemed*. I should like you to see her, and learn whether I may come back again as before, and whether she will see and talk to me as an old friend. Do as you think best."

———

"I got your letter this morning, and I kiss the rod, not only with submission, but with gratitude. Your rebukes of me and your defence of her are the only things that save my soul from hell. She is my soul's idol, and, believe me, those words of yours applied to the dear creature ('to lip a chaste one and suppose her wanton') were balm and rapture to me.

"Be it known to you, that while I write this, I am drinking ale* at the Black Bull, celebrated in Blackwood's. It is owing to your letter. Could I think her 'honest,' I am proof even against Edinburgh ale!

* He had not for years previously touched anything but water, except his beloved tea, nor did he afterwards, up to the period of his last illness.

She, by her silence, makes my 'dark hour,' and you dissipate it—for four-and-twenty hours.

* * * * * *

"I have seen the great little man,† and he is very gracious to me. I tell him I am dull and out of spirits, but he says he cannot perceive it. He is a person of infinite vivacity. My Sardanapalus is to be in.‡

"In my judgment, Myrrha is just like ——————, only I am not like Sardanapalus.

"Do you think if she knew how I love her, my depressions and my altitudes, my wanderings and my pertinacity, it would not melt her? She knows it all! I don't believe that any human being was ever courted more passionately than she has been by me. As Rousseau said of Madame d'Houdetot (forgive the allusion), my soul has found a tongue in speaking to her, and I have talked to her in the divine language of love. Yet she says she is insensible to it. Am I to believe her or you? You; for I wish it to madness."

———

"The deed is done, and I am virtually a free man.
* * * What had I better do in these circumstances? I dare not write to her—I dare not write to her father. She has shot me through with

† Jeffrey.

‡ An article in the Edinburgh Review on Byron's tragedy so called.

poisoned arrows, and I think another 'winged wound'
would finish me. It is a pleasant sort of balm she
has left in my heart. One thing I agree with you in
—it will remain there for ever—but yet not long. It
festers and consumes me. If it were not for my little
boy, whose face I see struck blank at the news, and
looking through the world for pity, and meeting with
contempt, I should soon settle the question by my
death. That is the only thought that brings my
wandering reason to an anchor—that excites the least
interest, or gives me fortitude to bear up against what
I am doomed to feel for *the ungrateful*. Otherwise,
I am dead to all but the agony of what I have lost.
She was my life—it is gone from me, and I am grown
spectral. If it is a place I know, it reminds me of
her—of the way in which my fond heart brooded over
her. If it is a strange place, it is desolate, hateful,
barren of all interest—for nothing touches me but what
has a reference to her. There is only she in the world—
'the false, the fair, the inexpressive she.' If the
clock strikes, the sound jars me, for a million of hours
will never bring peace to my breast. The light
startles me, the darkness terrifies me—I seem falling
into a pit, without a hand to help me. She came (I
knew not how) and sat by my side, and was folded in
my arms, a vision of love and joy—as if she had
dropped from the heavens, to bless me by some
special dispensation of a favouring Providence—to
make me amends for all. And now, without
any fault of mine but too much love, she has vanished

from me, and I am left to wither. My heart is torn
out of me, and every feeling for which I wished to
live. It is like a dream, an enchantment—it torments
me, and makes me mad. I lie down with it—I rise
up with it—and I see no chance of repose. I grasp
at a shadow—I try to undo the past, or to make that
mockery real—and weep with rage and pity over my
own weakness and misery.   *   *

"I had hopes, I had prospects to come—the
flattering of something like fame—a pleasure in
writing—health even would have come back to me
with her smile. She has blighted all—turned all to
poison and drivelling tears. Yet the barbed arrow
is in my heart—I can neither endure it nor draw it out,
for with it flows my life's blood. I had dwelt too
long upon Truth to trust myself with the immortal
thoughts of love. *That* ——— ——— *might have
been mine—and now never can :* these are the two
sole propositions that for ever stare me in the face,
and look ghastly in at my poor brain. I am in some
sense proud that I can feel this dreadful passion. It
makes me a kind of peer in the kingdom of love.
But I could have wished it had been for an object
that, at least, could have understood its value and
pitied its excess.   *   *   *   The gates of
Paradise were once open to me, and I blushed to
enter but with the golden keys of love! I would die
—but her lover—my love of her—ought not to die.
When I am dead, who will love her as I have done ?
If she should be in misfortune, who will comfort her ?

When she is old, who will look in her face and bless her?   *   *   *   Oh, answer me, to save me if possible *for* her and *from* myself!

"Will you call at Mr. ———'s school, and tell my little boy I'll write to him or see him on Saturday morning. Poor little fellow!"

———

"Your letter raised me a moment from the depths of despair; but, not hearing from you yesterday or to-day (as I hoped), I am gone back again. You say I want to get rid of her. I hope you are more right in your conjectures about her than in this about me. Oh, no! believe it, I love her as I do my own soul: my heart is wedded to her, be she what she may; and I would not hesitate a moment between her and an angel from heaven. I grant all you say about my self-tormenting madness; but has it been without cause? Has she not refused me again and again with scorn and abhorence?   *   *   *   'She can make no more confidences!' These words ring for ever in my ears, and will be my deathwatch. My poor fond heart, that brooded over her, and the remains of her affections, as my only hope of comfort upon earth, cannot brook or survive this vulgar degradation. Who is there so low as I? Who is there besides, after the homage I have paid her, and the caresses she has lavished on me, so vile, so filthy, so abhorrent to love, to whom such an indignity could have happened? When I think of this (and I think

of it for ever, except when I read your letters), the
air I breathe stifles me.   I am pent up in burning
impotent desires, which can find no vent or object.
I am hated, repulsed, bemocked, by all I love.   I
cannot stay in any place, and find no rest or
interruption from the thought of her contempt, and
her ingratitude.   I can do nothing.   What is the use
of all I have done ?   Is it not that my thinking beyond
my strength, my feeling more than I ought about
so many things, has withered me up, and made me
a thing for love to shrink from and wonder at ?   Who
could ever feel that peace from the touch of her hand
that I have done; and is it not torn for ever from me ?
My state is, that I feel I shall never lie down again
at night, nor rise up of a morning in peace, nor ever
behold my little boy's face with pleasure while I live,
unless I am restored to her favour.   Instead of that
delicious feeling I had when she was heavenly kind to
me, and my heart softened and melted in its own
tenderness and her sweetness, I am now enclosed in
a dungeon of despair.   The sky is marble, like my
thoughts; nature is dead without me, as hope is
within me; no object can give me one gleam of
satisfaction now, or the prospect of it in time to come.
I wander, or rather crawl, by the seaside; and the
eternal ocean, and lasting despair, and her face, are
before me.   Hated, mocked by her on whom my
heart by its last fibre hung.   I wake with her by my
side, not as my sweet companion, but as the corpse
of my love, without a heart in her—cold, insensible,

or struggling from me; and the worm gnaws me, and the sting of unrequited love, and the canker of a hopeless, endless sorrow. I have lost the taste of my food by feverish anxiety; and my tea, which used to refresh me when I got up, has no moisture in it.   Oh? cold, solitary, sepulchral breakfasts, compared to those which I made when she was standing by my side; my Eve, my guardian angel, my wife, my sister, my sweet friend, my all.   *   *   *   Ah! what I suffer now, shows only what I have felt before.

"But you say, ' The girl is a good girl, if there is goodness in human nature.'   I thank you for those words, and I will fall down and worship you, if you can prove them true; and I would not do much less to him that proves her a demon.

"Do let me know if anything has passed; suspense is my greatest torment.   I am going to Renton Inn, to see if I can work a little."

————

"I ought to have written you before; but since I received your letter I have been in a sort of hell. I would put an end to my torments at once, but that I am as great a coward as I am a fool. Do you know that I have not had a word of answer from her since? What can be the reason? Is she offended at my letting you know she wrote to me? or is it some new amour? I wrote to her in the tenderest, most respectful manner—poured my soul at her feet—and this is the way she serves me! Can you account for it, except on the admission of my worst suspicion? God! can I bear to think of her so—or that I am scorned and made sport of by the creature to whom I have given my very heart? I feel like one of the damned. To be hated, loathed as I have been all my life, and to feel the utter impossibility of its ever being otherwise while I live, take what pains I may! I sit and cry my eyes out. My weakness grows upon me, and I have no hope left, unless I could lose my senses quite. I think I should like this. To forget—ah! to forget—there would be something in that—to be an idiot for some few years, and then wake up a poor, wretched, old man, to recollect my misery as past, and die! Yet, oh! with her, only a little while ago, I had different hopes—forfeited for nothing that I know of."

———

"I was in hopes to have got away by the steam-boat to-morrow, but owing to * * * I cannot, and may not be in town till another week, unless I come by the mail, which I am strongly tempted to do. In the latter case, I shall be there on Saturday evening. Will you look in and see, about eight o'clock? I wish much to see you, and her, and John Hunt, and my little boy, once more; and then, if she is not what she once was to me, I care not if I die that instant."

———

Many of the letters in the "Nouvelle Héloise" are among the most beautiful and affecting effusions which exist in those works of fiction that concern themselves with sentiment and passion, rather than with incident and action. But, I venture to say, that there is nothing in the "Nouvelle Héloise" equal in passion and pathos to the foregoing extracts. And the reason is, that the latter are actual and immediate transcripts from the human heart. In this respect the letters from which these extracts are taken are, perhaps, more beautiful and touching than anything of their kind that was ever given to the world. But I am far from doubting that innumerable others exist, equalling them in all the qualities in which *they* excel; for real and intense passion levels all ranks of intellect, laughs learning and worldly wisdom to scorn, and invests the common-places of life with the highest attributes of poetry and eloquence.

Perhaps the published writings most resembling these letters in the depth and intensity of the passion they embody and convey, are the celebrated letters addressed by Mary Woolstoncraft to Imlay.

[P. G. PATMORE].

APPENDIX III.

          "London, January 17th [1822].

"SIR,

"Dr. Read sent the "London Magazine," with
compliments and thanks; no letters or parcels, except
the one which I have sent with the 'Magazine,"
according to your directions. Mr. Lamb sent for the
things which you left in our care, likewise a cravat
which was sent with them. I send my thanks for
your kind offer, but must decline accepting it. Baby
is quite well. The first floor is occupied at present;
it is quite uncertain when it will be disengaged.

"My family send their best respects to you. I
hope, sir, your little son is quite well.

        "From yours respectfully,

                  "S. WALKER.

"W. Hazlitt, Esq."

———

"It is well I had finished Colburn's work* before
all this came upon me. It is one comfort I have

* The second volume of "Table Talk."

done that. . . . I write this on the supposition that Mrs. H. may still come here, and that I may be left in suspense a week or two longer. But, for God's sake, don't go near the place *on my account.* Direct to me at the post-office, and if I return to town directly, as I fear, I will leave word for them to forward the letter to me in London—not in S. B. . . . . I have finished the book of my conversations with her, which I call 'Liber Amoris.'

" Yours truly,

" W. H.*

" Edinburgh, March 30.

"P.S.—I have seen the great little man,† and he is very gracious to me. *Et sa femme aussi !* I tell him I am dull and out of spirits. He says he cannot perceive it. He is a person of an infinite vivacity. My Sardanapalus ‡ is to be in. In my judgment Myrrha is most like S.W., only I am not like Sardanapalus.

"P. G. Patmore, Esq.,
" 12, Greek Street, Soho, London."

* I am quoting from the original autograph letter : in the printed copy the text differs.

† Jeffrey.

‡ The review of Byron's "Sardanapalus" in the "Edinburgh."

[April 7, 1822.]

"MY DEAR FRIEND,

"I received your letter this morning with gratitude. I have felt somewhat easier since. It showed your interest in my vexations, and also that you knew nothing worse than I did. I cannot describe the weakness of mind to which she has reduced me. I am come back to Edinburgh about this cursed business, and Mrs. H. is coming down next week. . . . A thought has struck me. Her father has a bill of mine for 10*l.* unhonoured, about which I tipped her a *cavalier epistle* ten days ago, saying I should be in town this week, and 'would call and take it up,' but nothing reproachful. Now if you can get Colburn, who has a deposit of 220 pp. of the new volume, to come down with 10*l.*, you might call and take up the aforesaid bill, saying that I am prevented from coming to town, as I expected, by the business I came about. . . . .

                                        "W. H.

"P.S.—Could you fill up two blanks for me in an essay on Burleigh House in Colburn's hands,— one, Lamb's Description of the Sports in the Forest: see *John Woodvil*,

    To see the sun to bed, and to arise, &c.;

the other, Northcote's account of Claude Lorraine in his Vision of a Painter at the end of his life of Sir Joshua ? . . . .

"FINAL.—Don't go at all. . . . . To think that I should feel as I have done for such a monster!

"P. G. Patmore, Esq.,

"12, Greek Street, Soho, London."

———

[Edinburgh, April 21, 1822.]

"MY DEAR PATMORE,

"I got your letter this morning, and I kiss the rod not only with submission but gratitude. Your rebukes of me and your defences of her are the only things that save me....Be it known to you that while I write this I am drinking ale at the Black Bull, celebrated in Blackwood. It is owing to your letter. Could I think the *love* honest, I am proof against Edinburgh ale....Mrs. H. is actually on her way here. I was going to set off home....when coming up Leith Walk I met an old friend come down here to settle, who said, 'I saw your wife at the wharf. She had just paid passage by the *Superb*.'....This *Bell* whom I met is the very man to negotiate the business between us. Should the business succeed, and I should be free, do you think S. W. will be Mrs.——? If she *will* she *shall;* and to call her so to you, or to hear her called so by others, will be music to my ears such as they never heard [!]......How I sometimes think of the time I first saw the sweet apparition, August 16, 1820!....I am glad you go on swimmingly with the N[ew] M[onthly]

M[agazine]. I shall be back in a week or a month.
I won't write to *her*.

[No signature].

"I wish Colburn would send me word what he is
about. Tell him what I am about, if you think it
wise to do so.

"P. G. Patmore, Esq.,
  "12, Greek Street, Soho, London."

––––––

[Between June 3 and June 9, 1822, but undated].

"MY ONLY FRIEND,

"I should like you to fetch the MSS., and then to
ascertain for me whether I had better return there or
not, as soon as this affair is over. I cannot give her up
without an absolute certainty. Only, however, sound
the matter by saying, for instance, that you are
desired to get me a lodging, and that you believe
I should prefer being there to being anywhere else.
You may say that the affair of the divorce is over,
and that I am gone a tour in the Highlands........
Ours was the sweetest friendship. Oh! might the
delusion be renewed, that I might die in it! Test
her through some one who will satisfy my soul I
have lost only a lovely frail one that I was not likely
to gain by true love. I am going to see K——, to
get him to go with me to the Highlands, and talk
about *her*. I shall be back Thursday week, to

appear in court *pro formâ* the next day ......
  " Send me a line about my little boy.

" W.H.

  " 10, George Street,
        " Edinburgh."

———

" Renton Inn, Berwickshire,
[June 9, 1822].

" MY DEAR PATMORE,

  " Your letter raised me for a moment from the
depths of despair, but not hearing from you yesterday
or to-day, as I hoped, I am gone back again. . . .
I grant all you say about my self-tormenting madness, but has it been without cause?   When I think
of this, and I think of it for ever (except when I
read your letters), the air I breathe stifles me. . .
I can do nothing.   What is the use of all I have
done?   Is it not this thinking beyond my strength,
my feeling more than I ought about so many things,
that has withered me up, and made me a thing for
love to shrink from and wonder at? . . . . My
state is that I feel I shall never lie down again at
night nor rise up of a morning in peace, nor ever
behold my little boy's face with pleasure, while I
live, unless I am restored to her favour. . . . I
wander, or rather crawl, by the sea-side, and the
eternal ocean, and lasting despair, and her face are
before me. . . . . Do let me know if anything
has passed : suspense is my greatest torment.   Jeffrey

(to whom I did a little unfold) came down with
100*l*., to give me time to recover, and I am going to
Renton Inn to see if I can work a little in the three
weeks before it will be over, if all goes well. Tell
Colburn to send the 'Table Talk' to him, 92, George
Street, Edinburgh, unless he is mad, and wants to
ruin me. . . . Write on the receipt of this, and
believe me yours unspeakably obliged,

"W.H."

———

[Renton Inn, Berwickshire,
June 18, 1822.]

"MY DEAR FRIEND,

"Here I am at Renton, amid the hills and groves
which I greeted in their barrenness in winter, but
which have now put on their full green attire, that
shows lovely in this northern twilight, but speaks a
tale of sadness to this heart, widowed of its last and
its dearest, its only hope. For a man who writes
such nonsense I write a good hand. Musing over
my only subject (Othello's occupation, alas! is gone).
I have at last hit upon a truth that, if true, explains
all, and satisfies me. You will by this time probably
know something, from having called and seen how
the land lies, that will make you a judge how far I
have stepped into madness in my conjectures. If I
am right, all engines set at work at once that punish
ungrateful woman! Oh, lovely Renton Inn! here I
wrote a volume of Essays; here I wrote my enamoured

follies to her, thinking her human, and that below
was not all the fiends. . . . By this time you
probably know enough, and know whether this
following solution is *in rerum naturâ* at No. 9, S.
B. . . . Say that I shall want it [the lodging] very
little the next year, as I shall be abroad for some
months, but that I wish to keep it on, to have a
place to come to when I am in London . . . If you
get a civil answer to this, take it for me, and send
me word. . . . Learn first if the great man of Pen-
maen-Mawr is still there. You may do this by
asking after my hamper of books which was in
the back parlour. . . . Tell her that I am free
and that I have had a severe illness.

"W.H.

"I would give a thousand worlds to believe her
anything but what I suppose. . . .

"P. G. Patmore, Esq.,
    "12, Greek Street, Soho, London."

———

[Edinburgh, June 25, 1822].

"MY DEAR AND GOOD FRIEND,

"I am afraid that I trouble you with my querulous
epistles; but this is probably the last. To-morrow
decides my fate with respect to *her*; and the next
day I expect to be a free man. There has been a
delay *pro formâ* of ten days. In vain! Was it not
for her, and to lay my freedom at her feet, that I

took this step that has cost me infinite wretchedness?
. . . . You, who have been a favourite with
women, do not know what it is to be deprived of
one's only hope, and to have it turned to a mockery
and a scorn.   There is nothing in the world left that
can give me one drop of comfort—*that* I feel more
and more.   . . .   The breeze does not cool me,
and the blue sky does not allure my eye.   I gaze
only on her face like a marble image averted from
me.   Ah! the only face that ever was turned fondly
to me!

"I shall, I hope, be in town next Friday at
furthest. . . . . Not till Friday week.   Write,
for God's sake, and let me know the worst.

"I have no answer from her.   I *wish* you to call
on Roscoe* in confidence, to say that I intend to
make her an offer of marriage, and that I will write
to her father the moment I am free (next Friday
week), and to ask him whether he thinks it will be to
any purpose, and what he would advise me to do.
. . . . You don't know what I suffer, or you
would not be so severe upon me.   My death will, I
hope, satisfy everyone before long.

"W. H."

* The gentleman who had married the sister, and was said
to be very happy in his choice.

PUBLISHER'S NOTE.

PUBLISHER'S NOTE

The composition and publication history of *Liber Amoris* are surprisingly complicated for such a small book. This note is merely intended to clarify the order of events, and to indicate the existence of additional background material in the shape of printed texts of Hazlitt's original letters and journal.

THE COMPOSITION OF *LIBER AMORIS*

The three sections of *Liber Amoris* were composed at different times and in different forms during 1822 and were carefully combined by Hazlitt into a single book in the spring of 1823.

Part I contains seven scenes, or conversations, and two letters to S——, written while Hazlitt was on his way to Scotland to start divorce proceedings. In mid-March he told his correspondent Peter George Patmore "I have begun a book of our conversations (I mean mine and the Statue's) which I call *Liber Amoris*. I was detained at Stamford and found myself dull, and could hit upon no other way of employing my time so agreeably." On March 30th he wrote that he had finished the book, and "It is very nice reading." The small calf-bound notebook which contains the original manuscript of this section, marked "Stamford 1822", was only recently discovered and sold at Sotheby's. Hardly a word was altered between the manuscript, which was later transcribed by Patmore, and the printed version. Resemblances between Part I and Hazlitt's letters to Patmore in Part II (e.g. "The Reconciliation" and "Letter I") show how he was moving between notebook and letters. He also copied into his notebook parts of the letters he was writing to Sarah Walker (the full version of the second letter "To the Same" was printed in *John Bull* in June 1823 as part of the critical attack on Hazlitt). Before publication

Hazlitt concluded Part I with the note from the blank leaf of "Endymion" and the quotation from *Troilus and Cressida*.

Part II has quite a different history. The letters "To C. P ——, Esq" are based on a series which Hazlitt wrote to Patmore from Scotland between early March and late July of 1822. Sarah Hazlitt arrived in Edinburgh on April 21st and the divorce was finalised on July 17th, and Hazlitt remained in Scotland during this period apart from a brief trip to London in May. Some months later he edited these letters – some dramatically, some hardly at all – in the manner described briefly below.

Part III has a different genesis again, adding to the puzzle of "spontaneity" versus "deliberate composition", which surrounds *Liber Amoris*. The three long letters "To J.S.K ——. " are addressed to Hazlitt's friend, the Scottish dramatist James Sheridan Knowles, at whose invitation he went to lecture in Glasgow, and with whom he went walking in the Highlands in May. No known originals exist, and it is believed that the letters were never sent, but were composed as a device to continue the story of the infatuation after Hazlitt had returned to London in the summer of 1822.

PUBLICATION HISTORY

The Liber Amoris, or the New Pygmalion was published anonymously by John Hunt in 1823. (The title page, which was reproduced by Le Gallienne in 1893 and is included in this edition, contained an oval vignette of the picture referred to in the first conversation.) It was reprinted in a "Bibliotheca Curiosa" edition in 1884 and then in 1893 in the edition reproduced here, with an introduction by Richard Le Gallienne, published by Elkin Mathews and John Lane. The text is an accurate rendering of the 1823 text. In addition to his introduction, which includes much biographical speculation and indicates the critical response to the book on first publication, Le Gallienne included appendices, containing extracts from Sarah Walker's journal and from Hazlitt's essays and letters but it must be pointed out that, as he makes clear, the extracts are from edited versions of the letters which had already been published by Patmore in *My Friends and Acquaintances* (1854) and by W.C. Hazlitt in *Memoirs of William Hazlitt* (1867).

In the following year Le Gallienne, who now turned to the manuscripts of the Patmore letters, published a quite different edition of 500 copies which was privately printed. This he described as *"The Liber Amoris*. . . with additional matter now reprinted for the first time from the original manuscripts". In it he followed a reprint of the 1823 text with what he called an "original version" of the text, using the manuscript letters, but transcribing them most inaccurately.

In the twentieth century the *Liber Amoris* was, of course, included in the collected *Works* edited by Waller and Glover in 1902 and by P.P. Howe in 1930-34. It was reprinted separately in a New Universal Library Edition of 1907 and appeared in the United States in a limited art edition in 1908. There is also the *Liber Amoris and Dramatic Criticisms* edited by Charles Morgan in 1948, and the text is included in *William Hazlitt: Selected Writings*, edited by Ronald Blythe in 1970.

THE BACKGROUND MATERIAL: LETTERS AND JOURNAL

1978 saw the publication of *The Letters of William Hazlitt*, edited by Hershel Moreland Sikes, assisted by Willard Hallam Bonner and Gerald Lahey. Bonner had a particular interest in the *Liber Amoris* letters and had edited *The Journals of Sarah and William Hazlitt* (1959). The *Letters* contains accurate texts of all known letters to Patmore and Sarah Walker and allows one to see how carefully Hazlitt used his correspondence as raw material for the book, keeping the feeling of a spontaneous outburst while rendering the tone more sentimental and philosophical, less rude and sensual.

On a minor level, a frequent practice is the dropping of everyday references of irrelevant chit-chat which distract from the emotional centre. Thus Letter VI (No. 109, *Letters*) loses the following passage, "Be it known to you that while I write this I am drinking ale at the Black Bull, celebrated in Blackwood. It is owing to your letter"; and so "I am proof against Edinburgh ale" endures rather sadly only as "I am proof against all hazards". Another very common practice is the softening or omission of strong or physical phrases and words. Thus in Letter VIII (No. 115) for example "madness" becomes "folly", "abhorrence" becomes "resentment", "continence" becomes "reserve", and "impotent" becomes "fruitless" while the vivid "I wander, or rather crawl by the sea-side" becomes merely "I wander".

While several letters are used almost verbatim, with the kind of minor changes mentioned above, others are split, re-ordered and cut. New reflections and thoughts are added in separate sections or are inserted into the letters. In particular Hazlitt makes no use of long sections which dwell on his obsession with Sarah" chastity, and his conviction of her innate lustfulness. For example, Letter X from "St Bees" is largely taken up with a moving Romantic effusion on loneliness and despair in the face of natural beauty – "without her hand to cling to, I stagger like an infant on the edge of a precipice." Yet the original (No. 116) letter, which shares the same first paragraph, goes on to pages of anguished sexual innuendo and doubt; beginning with the recording of a "kitchen conversation" at 9 Southampton Buildings:

Betsy. Oh! if those trowsers were to come down, what a sight there would be. (*A general loud laugh*)
Mother. Yes! he's a proper one: Mr. Follett is nothing to him.
Mr. Cajah. (aged 17) Then, I suppose he must be seven inches.
Mother W. He's quite a monster, He nearly tumbled over Mr. Hazlitt one night.
Sarah. (At that once, that still as ever dear name, ah! why do I grow pale, why do I weep and forgive) said something inaudible, but in connection.
Cajah. (Laughing) Sarah says . . .
Sarah. I say, Mr. Follett wears straps –
_____ [I ask you candidly whether on hearing this I ought not to have walked quietly out of the house and never have thought of it again.]

She also said to me the other evening when I told her (I don't know what) that "she had heard enough of that sort of conversation." No wonder, when she had heard for years this kind of kitchen-stuff. Who do you think this hero, this Hercules, this plenipotentiary was? Why, I recollect the person who once tumbled over me half drunk was this very Griffiths who keeps possession of his ten-shillings Garrett, in spite of an offer of marriage from *me*, and a hundred guineas a year for his apartment. Can there be a doubt, when the mother dilates in this way on codpieces and the son replies in measured terms, that the girl runs mad for size? Miss is small, and exaggerates dimensions by contrast. Misjudging fair! Yet it is she whom [I have] spared a hundred times from witnessing this consummation devoutly wished by the whole kitchen in chorus, after she has been rubbing against me, hard at it for an hour together, thinking to myself, "The girl is a good [girl] etc. and means no harm – it is only [her fondness] for me, not her lech after a man["] she taunted me the other night. "She a[ssured] me she had no affection for me [yet she] owned she had been guilty of [making confidences to] me, *viz.* one for whom she had – which were not to be repeated in future, they having been transferred to one whom her mother has singled out for her daughter's endearments. "A strappan youth, he taks the mother's eye!" If you know nothing to contradict this theory, ask somebody to verify it [or do] it yourself, if you like as [hastily] as possible in proving some things. But did I not overhear the conversation? [I will] stake my existence on it. Whenever I poked her up she liked me best; and I stupidly declined the *ultimate* outcome "Which I had treasured" —— alone. *Hinc illae lachrymae!* [Death, death, death. But then] When I said I should —— she sighed, as if she then felt she must —— fascination. This view of the thing —— forgave it for her in demure looks ——.
* [If I don't hear something good from you tomorrow, I shall send this letter post-paid.]

This strain continues at great length. The physical jealousy revealed in this June letter had already driven Hazlitt, from April onwards, to a drastic notion – of which he gives no hint in the finished *Liber Amoris* – that Sarah's chastity must be tested by someone else, a proxy seducer. In May he had written "TRY HER through (anyone) someone. E. for example, who will satisfy my soul I have lost only a lovely frail one that I was not like to gain by true love." (See *Letters* No. 110).

*The edge of certain pages have been torn away.

In July, after another long, condemnatory tirade, ("The bitch likes but nasty, the wilful, the *antipathetic*. That was why she pitched on me, because I was out of the ordinary calculation of love,") he wrote across the top of the first page his letter; "Get someone to try her or I am lost forever. To go and see E . . . there after [he had taken her] for the asking, would lift my soul from Hell. It would be sweet and full revenge. *You* must try her, if you like. Pity me. Pity. . . W." (No. 120).

Hazlitt's journal of March 4-16th, 1823, shows that several months later, while he was actually preparing *Liber Amoris* for the press, his determination to test Sarah had not faded. (The relevant journal entries from Appendix A, in the *Letters*). A friend of Hazlitt's, no longer E—— but F——, rented a room in Southampton Buildings. Sarah was still continuing her relationship with Tomkins, the lodger Mr C—— who caused so much misery in the book. Hazlitt recorded the verbal and physical encounters of each day until he believed F.s pursuit has reached the stage when he wrote:

I thought I am exculpated by all this. I asked F. if he wanted to take a girl into keeping would he allow her half a guinea a week to be his whore? and he said, No, for one might get girls that would have some conversation in them for that, and she had not. He thought at first she would not talk, but now he was convinced she could not. He asked what was to be done if she consented to come to bed to him. I said Why you had better proceed. He did not seem to like the idea of getting her with child, and I said I supposed he didn"t like to have a child by a monster, which he said was really his feeling. In this child-getting business we are however reckoning without our host, for she has evidently some evasion for that. It remains to be seen what her theory and practice on this subject are.

In the end the callous experiment turned back on its author: "F. is I think already in love with her and thinks she likes him and I shan't be able to get him to move." But by March 15th Hazlitt had so identified with "F." seeing both as victims rather than assailants, that he is determined to believe her behaviour inscrutable and ambivalent to all men:

Saturday, March 15. She did not come up in the morning and nothing was done but that as she put down the curtains at night, he kissed her and saying he was determined to give a good tickling for her tricks in running away from him the day before, put his hand between her legs on that evening. She only said "Let me go Sir", and retiring to the door, asked if he would have the fire lighted. She did not come up again. She was altered in her manner, and probably begins to make something. In lighting F. upstairs she waits for him to go first, and on his insisting on her leading the way, they had a regular scamper for it, he all the way tickling her legs behind. Yet she expressed no resentment nor shame. This is she who murdered me that she might keep every lodger at a proper distance. – I met Tomkins in the street who looks bad. I fancy we are all in for it; and poor F. will be over[head] and very [?] with her in another week.

March 16. Saw nothing of her in the morning, but asked her to tea – answered "she never drank tea with gentlemen," and was high. F. was in despair when returning home at dusk, he met my lady with her muff on going along Lincolns Inn Fields by herself. He saw [her] turn at the corner of Queen Street to go down towards the New Inn. Followed her – asked to accompany – she refused – and on his offering to take her arm, stood stock still, immoveable, inflexible – like herself and on his saying he could not then press her and offering his hand, she give it him, and then went on to her lover. I also am her lover and will live and die for her only, since she can be true to any one. F. met her brother at the door and said, "I just met your sister." "Why she is gone to her grandmother's." Let her [and then cross hatched up the right side of the page is:] be to hell with her tongue –. She is as true as heaven wished her heart and lips [to] be. My [own?] fair hell.

So ends the journal sequence which, with the original letters, provide such remarkable supplementary material to the *Liber Amoris*.

The Hogarth Press, 1985